Bridging
the

Confidence
Gap

Bridging the

HOW EMPOWERED WOMEN CHANGE THE WORLD

Confidence Gap

SHEENA YAP CHAN

Wall Street Journal Bestselling Author

WILEY

Published by John Wiley & Sons, Inc., Hoboken, New Jersey.
Published simultaneously in Canada.

For general information on our other products and services or for technical support, please contact our Customer Care Department within the United States at (800) 762-2974, outside the United States at (317) 572-3993 or fax (317) 572-4002.

Wiley also publishes its books in a variety of electronic formats. Some content that appears in print may not be available in electronic formats. For more information about Wiley products, visit our web site at www.wiley.com.

Library of Congress Cataloging-in-Publication Data is Available:

ISBN: 978-1-394-25761-4 (cloth)
ISBN: 978-1-394-25762-1 (ePub)
ISBN: 978-1-394-25763-8 (ePDF)

Cover Design: Paul McCarthy
SKY10099954_031225

*This book is dedicated to the queen in you who has lost her way.
Here's a reminder of your greatness.*

You're a Queen.

*Until you embrace your inner majesty, it's entirely possible that
you have been settling for a life of a lesser title and nobility.*

If you've forgotten your radiance…

It's time for you to rise.

It's time for you to awaken your native majesty.

*It's time to see yourself in a whole new light with
your crown shining bright.*

Contents

Introduction

The State of Women's Leadership and Confidence

"Are you ready to level up this year, or are you okay with all the mediocrity that you have currently?"

THIS POWERFUL QUESTION, posed by my friend and renowned "coach of coaches" Mark Anthony Bates, sparked a journey that led to the creation of this book and the revolutionary Queen Maker and Tao Queens programs. As an Asian woman who has navigated the complex landscape of personal and professional growth, I understand the unique challenges we face. But this book isn't just for Asian women—it's for every woman ready to break through barriers and claim her rightful place as a leader.

When he asked me this question, I was actually scared to say I was ready to level up because part of me still felt like I wasn't ready. Part of me still felt like I needed to hide because I thought there were women out there who did a far better job than me.

On the surface level, it may look like I have accomplished so much in life and I am grateful for every single accomplishment that I have achieved. I don't take my achievements lightly because it takes a lot of courage to do what I do, especially when I come from a culture where I was told to stay in the background and never make any noise.

To be honest, I am still scared to take it to the next level because I am not sure if I can handle it when I do get to the top. Success can be so frightening at times and for years I held myself back because of this fear. I also realize that if I continue to fear success, the real positive changes that I want to see for women will not come to fruition. And this is why I emphatically replied, *"I am ready to level up!"*

I knew why my friend asked me this specific question. It was because he's known me long enough to know that I was ready to level up in ways I never thought possible. If you have ever been afraid of success, you are not the only one. This is something that most women do not talk about. But it's necessary to talk about because, as women, we deserve all the success in the world.

When I was offered the opportunity to write a second book, I wasn't too sure if I was going to accept it. I mean, I already wrote one book, so why do I need to write another? Then the same question came back to me again, and I had to remind myself that I am being given this opportunity for a reason. I had to grab the opportunity to write this book because it is so needed. As of now, women are still facing huge gaps in all areas of life compared to men, and we need to figure out how women can overcome this, or learn how to turn these gaps into opportunities.

Truth is, I have still been playing small up until now. I know there is still so much in me that I can do to create a better tomorrow for so many women out there because it is needed. Even though in 2025, women still face so many gaps, which is why I decided to level up and write this book.

You decided to pick up this book because you are tired of living with mediocrity. You also want to level up in your career and life, but it can be challenging when you don't have the right support system. I totally get it! When you try to do things on your own, it can be scary to the point where you resist even trying. This is one of the reasons there are fewer women in leadership roles.

Now is the time to change all that, and it starts with how you perceive yourself. This book will be a guide for you in your journey to create more courage and confidence for yourself. It is packed with information that you can use to apply into your own life. You will understand why, as a woman, so much holds you back from your greatness. When you can learn to unpack all the things that are holding you back, you can start to find ways to solve it so that you can show up as your best self.

One of the main reasons I decided to say yes to writing this book was because of a report that I saw during the COVID-19 pandemic. The World Economic Forum indicated that while the gender gap is back to 2019 levels, the earliest that women will achieve gender parity is in 2154.[1] That's just under 130 years from now. We won't see it, our daughters won't see it, and even our granddaughters won't see gender parity.

Here are some other facts about what women are currently going through globally, from World Bank blogs:[2]

- One in three women worldwide experience physical or sexual violence by an intimate partner or sexual violence by a non-partner over the course of their life.
- The global gender gap in employment has been nearly stagnant for the past three decades.
- Women spend more time on unpaid domestic and care work.
- Over the last 25 years, women's participation in national parliaments has increased but is far from reaching equality.

This is terrible. As a woman, I do not want to wait that long to achieve gender parity. It is the mid-2020s and yet there are still so many things that need to be fixed. This is why it is crucial for women from all walks of life to see their potential, so we can speed up the number of years until gender parity will be achieved.

And yes, to undertake a task like this is daunting, but if you and I don't tackle this problem, who else will do it? I always believe that if I want things to change, it has to start with me. This is why writing this book is a necessity. It will serve as a guide for you to unpack all the things you have been going through in order to find solutions to build your courage and confidence to be the woman leader you are meant to be.

The best part is that you are not alone in this journey. I also have to level up and show up so that I can help current and future generations of women see that they are capable too. And you'll learn about the Queen Maker and Tao Queens programs, designed to provide ongoing support, resources, and a community of like-minded women committed to growth and success (more on that in the Chapter 8).

In this book, I will share many eye-opening statistics that you may be unaware of. We'll explore the double standards women face (Chapter 1), examine how imposter syndrome affects so many women—myself included (Chapter 2), take a deep dive on the gender confidence gap (Chapter 3), look at ways to develop courage (Chapter 4), see why self-promotion empowers women (Chapter 5), survey the confidence era (Chapter 6), study the benefits of having more women in leadership (Chapter 7), and—ready, fire aim—learn the formula for women's leadership (Chapter 8).

Some of the topics and stats you'll read will be uncomfortable because when one woman suffers, every woman suffers. So I want to prepare you in case the topics sometimes feel like too much, but they are important to touch on and are rarely discussed in mainstream media. Even writing about them was uncomfortable for me at times, but I know it's important to include the issues women all over the globe are facing in the present moment.

Too often women have not been seen as "leadership material" due to the simple fact of being a woman. This is why I work 100 times harder to show up and help other women see what is possible for themselves.

It's unfortunate that women are still fighting for progress and even sometimes fighting for the basic needs to live their life. It truly breaks my heart to know that girls and women in Afghanistan cannot even go to school or get a job, and that little girls in Asia are being trafficked into prostitution and slavery.

This is not what I want for women. I want better for us, and this is why I said yes to writing another book. This is just not about me; this is for every single woman who is feeling invisible or voiceless. Through this book, I want to show them that they can emerge from any situation they may be facing at this moment and thrive.

So I will ask you the same question that Mark Anthony Bates asked me not too long ago:

"Are you ready to level up this year, or are you okay with all the mediocrity that you have currently?"

Let's get started on leveling up your own journey.

1

The Double Standards That Kill Confidence

As A WOMAN, you face many challenges. Most of them can be a big confidence killer, such as the double standards you face on a daily basis. You might not even be aware that this is keeping you stuck at the position you're in right now, or holding you back from becoming the woman you are meant to be.

So what do we really mean by "double standard"? Here's a definition from Bored Panda:[1]

> The double standard definition states that it is a rule or a principle applied to different people or groups. The most prominent case of double standard examples to this day come from gender equality. What's usually okay for men, is not acceptable when done by women.

These double standards can make it challenging to be a woman because no matter what you do, it's a lose-lose situation. An excellent summation of this idea is American Ferrera's monologue in the *Barbie* movie:[2]

It is literally impossible to be a woman. You are so beautiful, and so smart, and it kills me that you don't think you're good enough. Like, we have to always be extraordinary, but somehow we're always doing it wrong.

You have to be thin, but not too thin. And you can never say you want to be thin. You have to say you want to be healthy, but also you have to be thin. You have to have money, but you can't ask for money because that's crass. You have to be a boss, but you can't be mean. You have to lead, but you can't squash other people's ideas. You're supposed to love being a mother, but don't talk about your kids all the damn time. You have to be a career woman but also always be looking out for other people.

You have to answer for men's bad behavior, which is insane, but if you point that out, you're accused of complaining. You're supposed to stay pretty for men, but not so pretty that you tempt them too much or that you threaten other women because you're supposed to be a part of the sisterhood.

But always stand out and always be grateful. But never forget that the system is rigged. So find a way to acknowledge that but also always be grateful.

You have to never get old, never be rude, never show off, never be selfish, never fall down, never fail, never show fear, never get out of line. It's too hard! It's too contradictory and nobody gives you a medal or says thank you! And it turns out in fact that not only are you doing everything wrong, but also everything is your fault.

I'm just so tired of watching myself and every single other woman tie herself into knots so that people will like us. And if all of that is also true for a doll just representing women, then I don't even know.

Have you ever felt this way as a woman? You are not alone. So many women deal with this but no one ever talks about it. It's important to understand this because we face so many confidence issues with all these double standards.

The Labels Women Face

Words are powerful. They can either make or break a person. How many times have labels hurt your confidence to move forward? When a woman forges her own path, it tends to be seen in a negative light instead of a positive one.

You may have heard these ideas before:

- Men are **assertive,** but women are **aggressive.**
- Women are too **pushy,** while men are **ambitious.**
- Men are **passionate,** but women are **shrill** or **hysterical.**
- Women are **stubborn,** while men are **determined.**
- Men are **persistent,** but women are **nagging.**
- Women are **bossy,** while men are simply **"the boss."**

When a woman takes action on her path to greatness, it tends to be seen as pushy, aggressive, or too much, but a man who takes the same action is celebrated for it and is seen as confident. Labels can prevent a woman from moving forward. It's important to get rid of the negative labels so that women can be seen as confident and courageous instead of aggressive and bossy.

When a woman speaks up against injustice, she is considered whiny and complaining. When a man speaks up, he is taken seriously. I have often seen women labeled complainers for speaking out, myself included. In an Instagram reel where I talked about the issues Asian women face, a list of hate comments told me that I was complaining about my issues and that I needed to shut my mouth. To be honest, I started getting PTSD when I got comment notifications on Instagram. I had to learn to work through this and know that this is part of the journey when you speak up as a woman.

Yes, it will take some time and effort for these negative labels to be dismantled but it's important to start somewhere. Nothing changes if nothing changes. This is why I constantly show up to events and on social media. Sometimes it just takes one person to lead the way so that others can see what is possible for themselves.

Yes, it is scary. I still get scared but I also realized that if I want things to change for the better, then I have to be the change. I will continue to show up so that one day these negatives labels for women will be gone for good.

Negative Stereotypes

As a woman, you will face negative stereotypes that can hurt your confidence. Culture plays a huge role in forming stereotypes, and women from every culture face some form of negative stereotype. I realized that when I was looking for candidates to be a co-author for our Women Who BossUp book series. I have spoken to many women from all walks of life and realized that although I may come from a different culture, I still face similar situations for the sole reason that I am a woman.

While women from different cultures are each subjected to their own set of negative stereotypes, the outcome is similar. It is hurtful and it causes more harm for women, ranging from sexual violence to death. These negative stereotypes can also hurt a woman's confidence to move forward on her path. It is important to dismantle all of these stereotypes so that we can create better representation for women from all walks of life.

Following are some examples of the negative stereotypes that women from different cultures still face today.

Asian Women

Asian women have been consistently seen as quiet, submissive, and obedient. Because of this negative stereotype, they are rarely found in leadership roles. Also, Asian women are usually seen as sex objects, which leads to women being trafficked as sex slaves, and little girls being forced to marry men as old as their grandfather or sold as mail order brides. These stereotypes are definitely hurtful, and it is important to dismantle them so Asian women can be seen as leaders in their own right.

Latina Women

Latina women are often considered feisty and spicy. Because of this negative stereotype, Latina women are often seen as sex objects and not taken seriously in leadership roles. The "spicy Latina" stereotype can also lead to sexual violence and harassment. It is important to stop using this term because it does so much harm to Latina women.

Black Women

Black women have stereotypically been seen as the "angry Black woman," especially in the workplace. This means that Black women are often perceived as short-tempered, bitter, overbearing, aggressive, loud, and more, which hurts them from being promoted in the workplace.

Indigenous Women

Indigenous women are often seen as sexual objects and as promiscuous. This negative stereotype can lead to sexual violence against Indigenous women and even to murder. An article in the *Guardian* detailed the violence that Aboriginal and Torres Strait Islander women have experienced:[3]

- They are more than three times more likely to experience violence than non-Indigenous women.
- They are 11 times more likely to die from an assault.
- They are 32 times more likely to be hospitalized from injuries received during an assault.

Middle Eastern Women

Middle Eastern women are often oppressed, viewed as weak and needing financial support from men. Many Middle Eastern countries have strict rules for women; in Iran, for example, there was a time when women were not allowed to drive cars. It is important to dismantle these negative stereotypes so that Middle Eastern women can be seen as strong and independent and capable of being leaders in their own right.

Ageism

If you're a woman in your 40s, 50s, 60s, and beyond, you have been told that you have hit a certain expiration date to do many things in life. Women certainly have been let go from jobs due to age.

In Canada, an anchor by the name of Lisa LaFlamme was considered one of the most popular female news anchors in the country. When she decided to let her gray hair grow out, Bell Media fired her, and then had to do a lot of damage control due to the backlash.[4] There were older male news anchors with gray hair in the same studio who have been there for years and had not been fired for that reason.

Ageism is definitely something women face. But the idea that women "expire" after a certain age is a myth and must be called out as one. So many women have been able to start or change careers in their 40s, 50s, 60s, and beyond.

I am in my 40s and everything I truly achieved was in this age bracket: I wrote my first book with a major publisher, traveled to Europe for the first time, and started my speaking career in my 40s.

There are women out there who have started businesses in their 50s and 60s and succeeded. Older women are ditching the hair dyes and embracing their gray hair to showcase that aging is beautiful. There was even a woman who made her Olympics debut at the 2024 Summer Games in Paris at the age of 58, which is just inspiring to see.

And the woman who's proven to the world that you can thrive at any age is the oldest tattoo artist, a woman from the Philippines by the name of Apo Whang-Od. In April 2023, she was *Vogue*'s oldest cover model when *Vogue Philippines* shared her story. The cover got worldwide recognition for capturing her true beauty and strength at the age of 106. I actually shared her cover on LinkedIn, and it has received over 29,000 likes from around the world.

The cover is beautiful. It captures the beauty of her wrinkles and her authentic self. It's rare for a fashion magazine like *Vogue* to showcase a woman like Apo Whang-Od. Fashion magazines usually showcase young models on the front cover, so seeing Apo Whang-Od was a breath of fresh air that opened the doors to highlighting more older women on the front cover of a magazine. In that same year, Martha Stewart was on the cover of *Sports Illustrated* rocking a bathing suit. Seeing these women thrive at their age is proof that age ain't nothing but a number.

Appearance

When it comes to appearance, women have to show up a certain way in order to be taken seriously. Most of the time men do not have to worry about that. A man can look like a hippie or wear a Hawaiian shirt and still be able to get funding for their startup company. If a woman decides to roll up in a Hawaiian shirt to seek funding, she would be denied instantly.

The ageism women experience extends to looking too *you*. Young-looking women won't be taken seriously in the workplace. I remember interviewing a young woman on my podcast who mentioned that she had to lie at her workplace about being older than she actually was so her co-workers would listen to her suggestions during meetings.

Women also are constantly judged for their appearance, whether business or personal. When it comes to weddings or other fancy occasions, it's not considered fashionably acceptable if a woman wears the same dress to more than one party; meanwhile, a man can wear the same suit over and over again without any judgment.

It also doesn't help that the media expects women to be perfect in every way, shape, and form, which is unattainable, and leads to low self-esteem and self-worth. Women definitely feel it more than men, in fact girls start feeling low self-confidence as early as nine years old due to body image issues.[5]

It's important to remember that you are beautiful just the way you are and that you are perfectly imperfect. Showing up as our authentic selves, especially on social media, is necessary so that our future generations will not start feeling low self-confidence at such a young age. Evidence suggests that women and girls feel self-conscious about how they look due to the media. A report from Gitnux mentioned the following:[6]

- Almost 94% of teenage girls are body shamed, per the National Report on Self-Esteem.
- 54% of women are dissatisfied with their bodies.
- 80% feel TV and movie images breed insecurities.
- Over half of girls and a third of boys aged six to eight want to be thinner.
- Around 50% of girls aged 13–17 are bullied due to appearance.
- 88% of teen girls compare themselves to media images; 40% of them do so frequently.
- 59% of adult women report self-esteem impact; 47% link body shaming to eating disorders.

These stats are pretty eye-opening about how many women and girls deal with low self-confidence. And if you are a female of a certain size, you are ridiculed and called names, which leads to eating disorders. Meanwhile, if a man has a "dad bod," he is celebrated for it and is considered attractive by society.

Colorism is also another factor that women face. If you have a darker complexion, you are seen as ugly. To be beautiful is to have lighter skin—an attitude prevalent all over the world. The whitening products business, which preys on women's insecurities and is already a multibillion-dollar industry, is predicted to reach over $16 billion by the year 2030, according to a Yahoo Finance article.[7]

This is why it's important to highlight that every woman is beautiful in her own skin, regardless of the color. Chelsea Manalo showcased this when she became the first Black Filipina to win the title of Miss Universe Philippines.[8] As someone who was born in the Philippines, I consider this a very big deal, because the country has conditioned women to believe that in order to be beautiful, you need to have pearly white skin. Whitening products are everywhere in the Philippines, from billboards along the big highways to celebrity endorsements. Seeing Chelsea win is a step in the right direction to showcase that having darker skin is beautiful as well.

It's wild how much women have to deal with when it comes to appearance. We get so much backlash for every single flaw. No wonder we deal with so many confidence issues.

Intelligence

Men tend to underestimate women's IQ. In the workplace, women's ideas often aren't taken seriously simply because they come from a woman. Even though there is no such thing as the smarter sex, women tend to be more modest while men tend to be more confident. In other words, men are not more intelligent than women; they are simply more confident in their abilities and therefore more likely to just go out and make it happen.

Something that always bothers me is that Hollywood actresses are often asked demeaning questions when discussing a certain character they are playing for a movie. Scarlett Johansson, a top performer in the industry, gets asked some of the silliest and most sexist questions about her movie roles. In a 2012 interview, when she and Robert Downey Jr. were promoting *The Avengers*, the interviewer asked Downey how he was able to shift his attitude for the movie. Johansson, meanwhile, was asked about her diet and how she was able to fit into the Black Widow suit.[9] If Johansson is getting these silly questions on a constant basis, imagine what actresses of color have to go through.

Another actress who was asked a ridiculous question is Youn Yuh-jung, a famous South Korean actress who gained popularity in Hollywood when she played the grandmother in the 2021 movie *Minari*. Youn won multiple awards for the film and even snagged an Oscar for Best Supporting Actress. After winning the Oscar, you might think that reporters would have better questions to ask her but unfortunately it was the total opposite. A female reporter actually asked Youn, "What does Brad Pitt smell like?"

Good thing Youn knows how to put reporters in their place. Her response? "I didn't smell him. I'm not a dog."

I laughed when I heard her answer, and then started cheering her on because men do not get silly questions like this. It's a slap in the face for Youn to be asked such a question and it's even worse that a woman asked it. Just because she is from Korea doesn't mean she is not capable of answering intelligent questions. This woman is a phenomenal actress and can speak English fluently, yet she is treated like she is stupid.[10]

Gender Pay Gap

Even at the end of the first quarter of the twenty-first century, the gender pay gap still exists. Men continue to be paid more than women for doing the same exact job and of course that can and does hurt a woman's worth. Sometimes I'm offered a fee for speaking engagements that is a fraction of what a male speaker would be paid to talk about the same subject matter. And sometimes organizations expect me to speak for free because I am a woman, while the men get paid to speak at the same event.

These are the times where it can be frustrating. It's not always rainbows and butterflies. It can be tough because even when you know what you're worth, it may take time to show others you deserve to be paid a certain amount, not only as a woman but as a woman of color. Even with all your accolades, you may still get shortchanged because of your gender and cultural background.

In an interview on YouTube, Viola Davis talks about a similar situation, being a woman of color in Hollywood. Viola Davis is a phenomenal actress who's been in the industry for over 30 years and is an EGOT winner (meaning she has won an Emmy, a Grammy, an Oscar, and a Tony). She is called the Black Meryl Streep by her peers but she definitely doesn't get the same pay as Meryl Streep. Viola Davis also mentions the pay disparity between actors and actresses in Hollywood. While a Caucasian actress might make half of what a Caucasian actor would make, women of color like Davis would probably get about a tenth of what a Caucasian actress makes. And on top of this, Viola Davis is number one on the call sheet, which means all the other actresses of color get paid much less than she does. You would think winning all those awards and having a track record like hers would guarantee instant, high-paying jobs, but in fact she still has to hustle to get the acting jobs she desires.[11]

It's not always easy to navigate situations like this. You may know your worth but are forced to take a lower fee or no pay because you should be "grateful" that you are given the opportunity. Yes, you have to start somewhere, but when do you say, "Stop—you need to pay me what I'm worth"? You did your time, you got the recognition, and you've put in the work, yet it seems like you're still in the same spot where you started. This situation happens in almost every industry. It's bad enough that women are paid less than men, and it's even worse for women of color, which can be very detrimental to self-confidence.

A report from Forbes Advisor offers some up-to-date general stats on the gender pay gap, as of 2024:[12]

- Women earn 16% less than men on average.
- Women earn just 84 cents for every dollar a man makes.
- Women of color are among the lowest-paid workers in rural areas, with rural Black and Hispanic women making just 56 cents for every dollar that rural white, non-Hispanic men make.
- Latinas are compensated at just 55% of what non-Hispanic white men are paid.
- Black women are paid 64% of what non-Hispanic white men are paid.

- Native American women are typically paid only 59 cents for every dollar paid to non-Hispanic white men.
- A 20-year-old woman just starting full-time, year-round work stands to lose $407,760 over a 40-year career compared to her male counterpart.

Imagine losing $407,760 in a 40-year career span! That is enough money to buy a house in many areas.

If companies started giving women equal pay or paid for their real worth, it would actually be more profitable for them. Most companies do not realize the buying power of women or that in a marriage, women make 80% of the buying decisions. And according to TechCrunch, women control and/or influence 85% of the consumer spending.[13]

A great example of a company that made big profits from women is Stanley Quencher, originally known for marketing beverage containers to men. As sales were dropping for the company in 2019, they decided to market to women by partnering with a women-run blog called The Buy Guide. Since then their sales have skyrocketed, from an average of $75 million annually to a projected review of $750 million in 2023.[14] That is a big pay raise for the company.

Another concept that affects a woman's pay is the motherhood penalty, which, according to *Fortune*, "is the price women pay for growing their families while they're in the workforce. Statistics show that moms in the workforce are less likely to be chosen for new roles and promotions, will earn lower salaries, and be held to a higher standard than fathers and non-mothers."[15]

Here are some specifics on how the motherhood penalty negatively affects women:

- Women make up almost half of the U.S. workforce and most are mothers.
- About 71% of mothers with children work from home.

- Women are the sole or primary breadwinner in 41% of American households with children.
- Research has shown that hiring managers are less likely to hire mothers compared to women who don't have kids, and when employers do make an offer to a mother, they offer her a lower salary than they do for other women.
- There's evidence that men actually receive a fatherhood bonus when they become dads.
- A study by U.S. Census Bureau researchers found that between two years before the birth of a couple's first child and a year after, the earnings gap between opposite-sex spouses doubles.
- 43% of women workers had at least one year with no earnings, nearly twice the rate of men.

It's time to pay women what they are worth!

Gender Gap in Venture Capital

Did you know that female-founded companies receive only about 2% of venture capital funding?[16] The VC world is still a male-dominated industry like so many other industries, but the disparity in funding between companies led by men compared to those led by women is quite large.

Women are lucky to even get $1 million in VC funding, while men receive 50 times that amount or more. On top of that, imagine how much more work a woman has to do to get even that fraction of funding that men get. Dealing with rejection after rejection can bring down your sense of confidence and self-worth thinking you are not good enough when it's the total opposite.

Of course, some bad apples ruin it for everyone. Elizabeth Holmes was probably one of the most successful female entrepreneurs when it came to securing funding but because she scammed many investors, every other female entrepreneur in the venture capital space is paying for her sins.

Meanwhile, Adam Neumann bankrupted his company WeWork and got a $1 billion severance package. He started a new company called Flow and received $350 million in funding in the process.[17] There were no real consequences for his actions, and men in the VC space haven't had to pay the price for his actions.

What Elizabeth Holmes did was definitely wrong, but it is unfair that women in the VC realm are being penalized for one woman's actions while men in that same space engage in questionable behavior and pay no real consequences for it.

It's important to realize that women are just as capable or even more capable than men in the VC space.

Bro Culture in the Workplace

It's no surprise that "bro culture" still exists in the workplace. Breathe HR describes it this way:[18]

> 'Bro culture' describes a culture that prioritises young macho men with obnoxious and toxic behaviour above all else. The average 'bro' tends to be a hustling guy who places winning and success above respect for others. 'Bros' operate in an environment of excessive partying and bullying. Harassment of colleagues is the everyday norm.

I have spoken to many women who have experienced this and it can really take a toll on a woman's mental health and confidence. I've heard horrifying stories from women who have been harassed, fired, sued, and more due to this toxic culture. A woman on LinkedIn shared her experience of attending a work event where she was drugged by her male colleagues. After having four drinks that were handed to her by her male colleagues in a span of three and a half hours, she ended up in the ER at 3 a.m. When she tried to file a report to her boss, not only did the company refuse to listen to her, but she was fired and the company filed a sexual harassment and substance abuse case on her.

This woman is fighting back and filed a lawsuit against her former employer for what they did to her. When I read her story on LinkedIn[19] I felt so much pain for her because of the trauma she continues to go through, as well as embarrassment on her behalf that this happened to her through no fault of her own. She is only one of many women who have been through similar situations, and many are too afraid to make their story public.

It's important for women share their stories because it might help someone else. If you have gone through a similar situation, know that you are not alone. More women have experienced this kind of thing than you might think. A report from Women in Tech Network found the following:[20]

> 72% of women in tech report experiencing a prevalent "bro culture" at work, signifying gender discrimination. Meanwhile, 63% of those in engineering and IT roles have encountered this pervasive bro culture, a rate slightly lower than that of women working in other tech-related departments.

It's disturbing to realize that bro culture is still prevalent in 2025. So many women have suffered from this toxic work environment, and it needs to be stopped. There's little point in companies creating programs to empower women when they cannot even help their women employees when it's needed the most. This type of behavior needs to end so that women are treated fairly and respectfully in the workplace.

Role of Men and Women

It's no secret that in the realm of traditional gender roles, women tend to be seen as the caregivers. For those who are not married, most women will always have someone to care for, whether it's their children or their parents. And women are expected to fulfill the caretaker role while working a full-time job or running a business. It's exhausting, and it's been normalized in society.

Men rarely have to live with these same expectations. And in the rare instances when they *are* the primary caregiver, they receive accolades as the stay-at-home dad—for taking care of their own children. Why are they praised for doing the same exact thing that women are expected to do thanklessly all the time?

I remember listening to someone with a very big influence online who always mentions that in order to succeed in your business, you must hustle 12 hours straight every day to make it happen or else you are a failure. For a while, I believed him. I really thought I was a failure because I didn't work 12 hours straight every day on my business. But then I realized that this is not the only thing I'm doing. I also have to run errands for my parents and babysit my nieces, along with working a full-time job at that time. So I don't need to feel bad for myself because I do not have the same opportunities as this person of influence, who could afford the luxury of working 12 hours a day because he wasn't running the household or taking care of kids.

Women are lucky if they can squeeze in a couple of hours to work on their business each day. If we had 12 hours a day to ourselves, imagine what we could do! I stopped listening to that influencer because he made me feel bad if I didn't constantly hustle. Yes, it's important to hustle in spurts, but you also have to take time to rest and recharge. You are not productive if you are constantly hustling without breaks.

When Women Are the Problem

Unfortunately, women can also have double standards for other women. How many times have you judged another woman for what she's wearing, or because more of her friends are guys rather than girls?

This may be a hard pill to swallow because it is rarely talked about. But it needs to be addressed because part of the reason women aren't advancing as fast is, well, us. I once worked in an office where the women at my job hated me. They excluded me in work-related events, I constantly got in trouble for the smallest things, and they were rude to me when I talked to them. It was difficult because I wondered what I did that made them treat me this way, but I couldn't pinpoint anything other than basic resentment or because I was a lot younger than they were. I'm sure you have dealt with women like that in your workplace as well.

A friend asked me for some advice. She had reached out to her boss's boss and asked to go out for coffee. The person said yes but all her female coworkers were telling her to cancel because they thought it was a bad idea on her part. She wanted to know if she should move forward with it or cancel. I told her to move forward with the coffee chat, because he had already said yes and if she backed out, that person would not take her seriously. I was happy that she was able to move forward with the coffee chat.

I have also heard stories of women who reach top positions but don't bring other women with them or support them in their career ambitions. This scarcity mindset needs to change because there's more than enough room at the top. So many women have told me that they were very disappointed when a woman in a high position became the one sabotaging their career.

Melissa Weaver posted a TikTok video saying she was allegedly denied a job as vice president in a human resources department by the recruiter because she didn't wear makeup during the interview. The recruiter was a woman. During the interview, Weaver did everything right. She wore the right clothes and the interview went 10 minutes longer than scheduled. She thought she had a great chance of getting the job but she received an email stating that the company would not be moving forward with her. When Weaver asked the recruiter what the reason was, the recruiter said that she did not put enough effort in her appearance for the interview. The TikTok video went viral and was viewed over 266,000 times, with many people in the comments siding with Weaver.[21]

Even as an entrepreneur, you join certain women's groups thinking you'll get the support you need in your business, only to be disappointed because they bring you down instead of lifting you up. I have witnessed this many times, so I choose wisely which groups I situate with and who really wants what is the best for you. I am grateful to have two women's groups that have a genuine heart for elevating women. Without them, I would not be here today.

What about if you're a mom? How many times have you dealt with "mom guilt" from other women? If you're working a job, you may be considered a bad mom because you're not at home taking care of the kids, and being shamed for that can be a huge confidence killer. It's important to give grace to others; everyone is trying their best to make it work, so instead of shaming them, we should be each other's support. Do we shame dads for working and not taking care of their children? Of course not.

Every culture has double standards. Being a single Asian woman in my 40s, I deal with it all the time. When I tell people I'm single and have never been married, people look at me like I'm an outcast or something is wrong with me, which is pretty typical in Asian culture. What's worse are the married women who look down on you, deeming you socially awkward because you are still a single woman in your 40s and beyond.

For the longest time I felt like a failure because I wasn't married, even though I was able to write a book, have an award-winning podcast, and speak on stages all over the world. I measured my worth by my marital status, which was wrong.

I have aunties and uncles at parties who tell people they were so relieved that all of their children are married off and they have no single kids. It was kind of a slap in the face to hear that, and that should not be the ultimate goal for your children. What happens if their children are in a loveless marriage or their spouse is violent with them? Is it still a better situation to be married off than to be single?

I remember when I accepted a friend request from an old friend from high school, and the first thing he said to me was "You're still single, I thought you'd be married by now." In that moment, I felt like a loser because most of my high school friends were married and I was still single with no prospects, and I really thought something was wrong with me. Why couldn't I get a man? Did I do something to repel them? So many questions were running through my head and I had to mentally slap myself. I was able to do so many things that most people couldn't even dream of, but I was focusing on the wrong things.

Even as recently as summer 2023, I unexpectedly saw an ex-boyfriend at a food festival with his current girlfriend. At first I felt bad about myself because he was with someone and I was still alone with no prospects. I threw myself a pity party until I realized that if I had stayed with him, I wouldn't have been able to live in Hawaii for two winters, stay in the Philippines for months at a time, travel to other parts of the world, start a podcast, become a *Wall Street Journal* bestselling author, and more, because I would have been so invested in him that I would have dropped everything just to be with him. After seeing it from that perspective, I felt better about myself and what I have accomplished. I have learned to let this go. If I find someone who I can spend the rest of my life with, that's great. If I end up single, that is fine as well. I will still live my life to the fullest regardless of the circumstances. I am still loved by my family, my friends, and, most importantly, *myself*!

To be honest, this is the stuff that I would normally never reveal, but I think it's important to share because I know there are other women out there who are feeling the same way, but you need to understand that there is nothing wrong with you; the women who make you feel that way are the ones who are wrong. Everyone is on a different life path, and we need to enjoy the journey.

It's important to be with someone you love for the right reasons and not because you're afraid of being alone. I have seen women stuck in situations because they think it's better to be with the wrong person than to be unmarried. I may not be an expert on relationships but I do know that I love myself just the way I am and I believe that everything will fall into place.

Perhaps the worst of it all is when women with power abuse it and prey on younger women for their personal gain. A great example is Ghislaine Maxwell, the socialite who is well known as Jeffrey Epstein's ex-girlfriend who used her status to recruit young girls to be sexually abused by Epstein. It's unsettling to see women taking advantage of young girls like that and putting them through trauma. The Netflix documentary about Maxwell makes it clear that the women she targeted are still traumatized by what happened. But it's heartening that these women had the courage to share their story so that other victims of sexual abuse will not be shamed into these kinds of situations. Ghislaine Maxwell is currently serving a 20-year sentence for her crimes but is now appealing her case.[22]

This part may be hard for you to read yet it's necessary to understand. It may be considered taboo to talk about women being mean to other women, but it happens, and we need to be aware so we can find ways to solve this problem. I always believe that when women work together for the common good, we become unstoppable, and that is why I decided to share this. I want us to stop bringing each other down and instead start finding ways to lift each other up.

Social Status

When it comes to social status, usually the more money you have, the more you can get away with. A prime example is Harvey Weinstein. For years he used his power to seduce and abuse women, promising them fame and fortune in Hollywood. If women denied him, he would derail their careers.

Mira Sorvino rejected Harvey Weinstein's sexual advances at least three times, and consequently her career suffered. She started noticing that she wasn't being offered any major roles and started doing more indie films and television. Sorvino never measured her worth as an actress but instead measured it by being a good person. Even though her acting career was derailed, she has a loving family and has been a UN Goodwill Ambassador in Human Trafficking since 2009.[23] And Sorvino certainly isn't the only woman who rejected Weinstein and suffered the consequences in their acting career.

Weinstein is one of the many examples of men who have abused their money and power for personal gain and have done so much damage to so many women. Some of these women will never get justice, and I pray that they are able to work through their traumas.

Sexual Assault

Women face sexual assault at much greater rates than men do. Here are some statistics from Plan Street about sexual assault in America:[24]

- 91% of rape and sexual assault victims are women.
- Over 50% of women and one in three men have experienced sexual violence involving physical contact during their lifetimes.
- Around 81% of women and 43% of men have experienced some type of sexual harassment in their lifetime.
- Approximately 74.9% of bisexual women, 43.3% of heterosexual women, and 46.4% of lesbians reported having experienced sexual violence at some point.
- Rape rates in the United States are unacceptable, with an estimated 1 in 10 women having been raped by an intimate partner.
- American Indians are twice as likely to be victims of rape and sexual assault as compared to other races.
- The Department of Defense estimates that 8.1% of women serving in the military experience sexual assault.
- 55% of assaults occur at or near the victim's home.
- 5% of women report sexual violence from someone in the workplace.

- Girls and young women aged 16–19 are four times more likely to be victims of sexual assault than the general population.
- 1 in 9 girls and 1 in 20 boys will be sexually assaulted before the age of 18. The prevalence of assault among this age group is particularly concerning because this is society's most vulnerable population.

This is just in the United States. What about the rest of the world? In many countries sexual assault is accepted due to religion or cultural upbringing, which leaves women with so much trauma to work with.

An example is in Iran under Sharia law. The legal age for a girl to get married is 13 and can even be younger as long as their male guardian approves of the marriage.[25] Once a young girl is married to a much older man (sometimes old enough to be her grandfather), she is forced to have sex with him since she is treated as property. Yes, this is hard to read, but this is the reality for little girls with strict rules that cater to men.

During the 2022 "Woman Life Freedom" uprising in Iran, the security forces used rape and other forms of sexual violence to break women's spirits. According to a 120-page report from Amnesty International, many victims of this ordeal were gang raped. Men, women, and children as young as 12 years old faced sexual violence from Iranian authorities in an effort to silence them. The security forces that took part in these heinous acts were agents from the Revolutionary Guards, the paramilitary Basij force, and the Ministry of Intelligence, as well as different branches of the police force, including the Public Security Police, the Investigation Unit of Iran's police, and the Special Forces of the police.[26] It's really heartbreaking when you hear stories like this, which were hardly mentioned in mainstream media.

Something that is not talked about enough but is still happening today is the genocide of Yazidis, which has been happening since 2014. ISIS targeted the Yazidis, a Kurdish-speaking religious minority, and kidnapped many of the women from their families to use them as sex slaves. The terrorist group forced the women to convert to Islam; if they refused, they were raped, or even beaten to death. When ISIS decided to attack the Yazidis, it resulted in the following:[27]

- 1,268 Yazidis were murdered.
- 2,763 children became orphans.
- 6,417 women and girls were forced into sexual slavery and labor.
- 400,000 people were displaced, forced to live in refugee camps in Iraq and Syria.

And yet this is not talked about enough in the mainstream media. Not once have I ever heard of Yazidis and what they had to endure because of ISIS. It's really horrifying to hear that it's been happening for over 10 years and not once has it been brought to the attention of the world. How could the world ignore such a terrifying event that is still present today?

Religion

Many religions cater to men and affect women in a negative way, even sometimes leading to death. Sharia law is an interpretation of a religion that places strict rules on women for how they must act, what they must wear, and so on, and thus strips away a woman's freedoms.

Here are some of the rules that Sharia law places on women:[28]

- A girl's clitoris should be cut (Muhammad's words, Book 41, Kitab Al-Adab, Hadith 5251).
- Girls can be sodomized until eight years of age and vaginally raped after that.
- A woman or girl who has been raped cannot testify in court against her rapist(s).

- Testimonies of four male witnesses are required to prove rape of a female (Quran 24:13).
- A woman or girl who alleges rape without producing four male witnesses is guilty of adultery.
- If a woman or girl is found guilty of adultery, it is punishable by death.
- A male convicted of rape can have his conviction dismissed by marrying his victim.
- Muslim men have sexual rights to any woman or girl not wearing the hijab.
- A woman can have one husband, who can have up to four wives; Muhammad can have more.
- A man can beat his wife for insubordination (Quran 4:34).
- A man can unilaterally divorce his wife; a wife needs her husband's consent to divorce.
- A divorced wife loses custody of all children over six years of age or when they exceed it.
- A woman's testimony in court, allowed in property cases, carries half the weight of a man's.
- A female heir inherits half of what a male heir inherits.
- A woman cannot speak alone to a man who is not her husband or relative.

The sad part is that there are many countries in the world that enforces these so-called laws on women, including Pakistan, Iran, Ghana, India, Saudi Arabia, and more. This completely strips away a woman's voice and her freedom to live her own life.

It's a shame that this still happens right now. Afghanistan reenforced Sharia law on women when the Taliban took over the country in 2021. Even though the Taliban claimed that women's rights would not be stripped away, it was more of a PR campaign to win over the world after taking over the country. A Taliban spokesperson said they would even allow women to be in government, but not a single woman has been able to fill that so-called position to date.[29]

Other religions may not be as extreme as Sharia law but they still have an impact on women rights. The Catholic Church has never ordained a woman as a priest. While some changes have been made, such as allowing women to give and serve at the altar, the priesthood is still reserved only for men. These two Bible verses from the New International Version describe the role of women in the church:

> Corinthians 14:34-35: "Women should remain silent in the churches. They are not allowed to speak, but must be in submission, as the law says. If they want to inquire about something, they should ask their own husbands at home; for it is disgraceful for a woman to speak in the church."
>
> Timothy 2:11-12: "A woman should learn in quietness and full submission. I do not permit a woman to teach or to assume authority over a man; she must be quiet."

A woman must be quiet and be in full submission? That doesn't sit well with me. The Bible is the oldest and most popular book in the world and has been passed down for many centuries. Think about how many women have been silenced just by these words.

Fundamentalist and Evangelical churches view women as subordinate to men. The role of men is considered the dominant one, while women are presented with fewer opportunities in leadership positions.[30]

These are just a few examples of the negative ways that religion can affect women. I hope one day we can create a new belief system that will empower women.

Cults

Cults are also very dangerous for women. So many women have been recruited just to be abused by the cult leader. This pattern is made clear in the many Netflix documentaries on cults. It's even worse when the women are the ones recruiting for their leader. Allison Mack from the TV show *Smallville* went to prison for trafficking girls into the NXIVM cult. She manipulated innocent women to become sex slaves for the cult leader, Keith Raniere.[31] This is also a reminder that although cult leaders are generally men, there have also been some women-led cults preying on innocent women for personal gain.

Jung Myung-seok, who is currently in prison, also used his position as a leader in a cult for personal gain. He is the leader of the Jesus Morning Star (JMS) and would tell people he was Jesus Christ reincarnated. He also sexually abused many women through his organization. The Netflix documentary series based on him is called *In the Name of God: A Holy Betrayal.*[32]

Women who are part of cults are usually the leader's sex slaves, child brides, or sister-wives. The abuse they receive mentally and physically is heartbreaking. These so-called leaders prey on their insecurities to lead them to join their special group, only to be tormented, used solely for the leaders' personal gain in the name of religion.

The repression and double standards women face can be very challenging, but it's important to find a way to turn these gaps into opportunities for you to rise as a leader. You can start by checking out taoqueens.com to begin your journey to greatness.

Now it's time to talk about another topic that every woman deals with, myself included: the issue of imposter syndrome.

2

Imposter Syndrome: Changing the Narrative for Women

EVERYONE EXPERIENCES IMPOSTER syndrome at some point in their lives, but women suffer from it more than men do. Even as someone who writes and talks about self-confidence and leadership, I still face imposter syndrome.

In fact, when I was presented with the opportunity to write my first book, *The Tao of Self-Confidence: A Guide to Moving Beyond Trauma and Awakening the Leader Within*, I almost turned it down because I kept asking myself if I was the right person to talk about confidence and leadership, especially for Asian women. I felt like there were other women who would be better at writing about the subject. If one of my mentors hadn't encouraged me to seize the opportunity to write that book, I wouldn't have done it, nor would I be writing this second book.

Even when I was approached to write this book, I still had my doubts. I wondered whether the publisher had made a mistake. They really want me to write another book!? But of course, if I didn't seize this opportunity, I would be a hypocrite. It's easy to talk about confidence and leadership, but to actually walk the walk can be difficult, uncomfortable, and challenging at times.

I often wondered why women experience imposter syndrome so frequently, so I realized it was important to devote a chapter to it. When you understand the root cause of imposter syndrome and are able to overcome or reduce its frequency, you can show up as your best self. So let's take a deep dive into the issue of imposter syndrome.

What Is Imposter Syndrome?

According to BetterUp, psychologists Pauline Rose Clance and Suzanne Imes coined the term "imposter syndrome" in 1978. Here is their definition:

> Imposter syndrome is the condition of feeling anxious and not experiencing success internally, despite being high-performing in external, objective ways. This condition often results in people feeling like "a fraud" or "a phony" and doubting their abilities.[1]

Have you ever felt like a fraud or a phony even though you have achieved so much in your lifetime? Does part of you still feel like you're not good enough, you constantly doubt yourself, or you feel like there's someone else who can do it better? This means you have experienced imposter syndrome, and you're not the only one who feels this way.

In fact, an article in *Forbes* mentioned that 75% of female executives go through imposter syndrome in the workplace. Even though these executives have the education, training, and certifications as proof that they merit the job, they still wonder if they are qualified for the position because they feel inadequate or they experience self-doubt. The imposter syndrome these female executives go through results in working long hours, fear of asking for help or even of asking questions, apprehension over speaking up, and reluctance to take on more challenging roles.[2]

According to an article from Human Resources Director America, online searches for imposter syndrome surged to 75% in 2024, which is alarming. Here are the industries with the highest cases of imposter syndrome:[3]

- Creative arts and design (87%)
- Environment and agriculture (79%)
- Information research and analysis (79%)
- Law (74%)
- Media and internet (73%)

And women are more negatively affected by imposter syndrome than men are. A case study done by Hewlett Packard found that when it comes to applying for jobs, men who believe they are 60% qualified for a job will apply for that job, yet women want to feel they are 100% qualified before applying for the job.[4] This is pretty eye-opening, and I am guilty of this as well. I always feel like I need to be 100% ready to start a new project or reach out to potential clients. But waiting for conditions to be 100% right is an illusion. The best time to start your journey is *now*!

The Negative Effects of Imposter Syndrome

Imposter syndrome can affect you in such a negative way that it stops you from moving forward in your own journey. It is important to examine and talk about these negative effects so you can find a way to overcome them and show up as your best self.

You Hold Yourself Back

Of course, the experience of imposter syndrome tends to hold you back, and you resist taking action in your own journey. You end up not taking the opportunities that were meant for you because you believe there must be someone better for the job. It's such a shame because I believe women can be very successful when provided with the right tools and mindset to win.

Mental Health

Imposter syndrome can also negatively affect your mental health, potentially causing depression and anxiety. Your insecurities can also make you feel like a fraud because you underestimate yourself, your value, and your abilities. You may end up keeping all your feelings bottled up inside you because you don't want others to know that you are working through what you are feeling. This can lead to excessive alcohol use or taking drugs. If your mental health is declining, it's important to connect with a licensed mental health professional to work through it. And I want you to realize that you are more capable than you know.

Fear of Failure

Do you constantly worry about failing? I used to. Until my 30s I thought I was a perpetual failure and never wanted to try anything. This fear of failure stemmed from my childhood when I failed kindergarten for coloring outside the lines. Well into adulthood I didn't even try to succeed because I just felt like a fraud. But failure is not final; it's actually just feedback that you can use to course-correct along the way.

You Become More Insecure

Insecurity can be a huge problem. As women, we tend to overthink the situation to the point that we end up not taking an offer or not even taking the first step toward our greatness. The insecurity becomes so loud in our head that we end up being miserable because we didn't have the confidence to move forward and see our potential. A study conducted by OnePoll revealed that people typically feel insecure five times a day.[5]

The Need for Perfection

As women, we tend to want perfection. When you start a business, you are constantly delaying your launch because you're waiting for everything to be completely perfect, but if you do that you will be waiting a really long time. I know because I was one of those people who always delayed starting new projects because it wasn't "the right time" or it "wasn't perfect." Had I just launched and course-corrected as I went, I would have gotten the results I was seeking in the first place.

The quest for perfection affects women more than men. The "perfect" altered images we see in magazines, in movies, and on Instagram put so much pressure on women. It's time to dismantle this concept that women have to be perfect and teach women how to take imperfect action.

Self-Sabotage

Are there times when you become your own worst enemy? You constantly put yourself down and compare yourself to your peers, thinking they are better than you. I know it's easy to bring yourself down and pinpoint all your perceived flaws. This is why it's important to treat yourself like you'd treat your best friend. You would never tell your best friend that she's ugly or that she isn't qualified for a certain job she wants to apply for. If you treat your best friends like family, then it's important to start treating yourself as your own best friend. Keeping yourself from self-sabotaging isn't easy, of course, but your future self will thank you.

Types of Imposter Syndrome and Ways to Overcome Them

Now that we understand some of the negative effects of imposter syndrome, let's explore the different kinds of imposter syndrome and the ways you can be more aware when you start to experience them.

There appears to be seven types of imposter syndrome. The first five explanations (the Perfectionist, the Superhuman, the Natural Genius, the Soloist, and the Expert) are from Choosing Therapy, a website that curates evidence-based online mental health articles.[6] The other two definitions (the Noticer and the Discounter) come from the coaching platform BetterUp.[7]

The Perfectionist

The Perfectionist always hopes to attain the unattainable. You set such impossibly high standards for yourself that you end up bringing your confidence down when you can't achieve them. When you're constantly seeking to be flawless, your productivity is reduced and your anxiety increases. As a perfectionist, you want to be in control of everything by micromanaging others. You obsess about every little detail, you're afraid to make a mistake for fear of failure, and it becomes hard for you to make a decision.

To overcome this type of imposter syndrome, it's important to learn to let go of perfection. I know that it's easier said than done, but it's important to be okay with imperfections. Instead of aiming for perfection, learn to aim for progression. As I tell myself all the time, "Practice makes *progress!*"

Even though perfection can be the biggest confidence killer, it can be difficult for women to let that go. But when you realize that perfection is a myth and no one is perfect, you can go out there and forge your path. It took a while for me to learn to let go of perfection because I was raised to be perfect in everything I do. And to be honest, that is exhausting. So I continue to show up as imperfect so that other women can see that they are not alone in this journey.

Instead of taking big leaps, learn to take small actionable steps toward your goals. I always remind myself that Rome was not built in a day and neither are you. This is a journey and a process, so learn to love that and learn to love the mistakes you make along the way. I want you to realize that there is no such thing as perfection, and you being your imperfect self is what makes you beautiful inside and out.

The Superhuman

I hadn't realized that there was something even higher than being a perfectionist, but there is a concept known as Superhuman. This totally makes sense especially in the context of the culture I grew up in because I was always taught to be the best in everything, to be number one, and to be a very high achiever.

The Superhuman imposter syndrome means you want to be able to excel in every single thing you do, and that is extremely exhausting. Just like the impossibility of being perfect at what you do, you simply cannot be good at everything. Yet no matter what you do, you always feel like it's never enough, and therefore you continue to do more. It's truly unattainable to think that women can do it all. When women learn to ask for help and to help each other out, that's how we start creating more change for the better. As a Superhuman, you tend not to handle feedback well from others, you feel stressed when you are not working, you feel guilty if you decide to take a break or rest and recharge (which is totally necessary for your soul), and you put so much pressure on yourself to be the best at everything.

Women have been programmed to be the Superwoman for everything and for everyone in everything we do, but this is unattainable! We cannot possibly do every single thing, and that is okay.

To overcome this type of imposter syndrome, it's important to set aside some self-care time. You don't always have to be on the go. (I know, that's easier said than done.) You feel like once you reach your goal, you have to move onto the next one or else you'll feel like you are not worthy. It's okay to take a break and enjoy the moment. Know that you are more than enough no matter what situation you're in. It's essential to take care of yourself and celebrate your accomplishments.

When my first book made it to the *Wall Street Journal* bestseller list, I was ecstatic. First off, there were eight men on the list and two women: me and Brené Brown. So yes, it was a big deal. I was over the moon, sharing it all over social media, and people were sending me messages to congratulate me.

Then as the weeks passed by, I started getting depressed because I didn't know what to do with myself. I felt like I had to make another move to feel whole and important, instead of just enjoying the moment. So many people kept asking me what my next move was that sometimes I would freeze up because I actually had nothing planned but I felt like I was obligated to have that next move after hitting the bestseller list. Finally, when I got asked that question during a podcast interview, it was refreshing to have the confidence to say, "I don't know." I didn't die and the interviewer just moved on to the next question.

I was never taught to celebrate my achievements. Once I hit the goal, I just went on to the next one, then the next one, and so on. Nobody ever told me I needed to be in the moment and just be happy for what I achieved because it was a big deal to celebrate it. It can be difficult to do that when you have been taught to be a high achiever and to be on the go at all times. So remember that self-care is extremely important, and recognize that being Superhuman is not achievable.

The Natural Genius

The Natural Genius form of imposter syndrome means that you believe your success is based on your natural talent or innate intelligence. As a Natural Genius, you think that success always comes easy because you don't have to try so hard. As a result, you end up setting impossibly high standards—which of course are unattainable. When a Natural Genius does end up in that impossible area, they feel like they have to force themself to the challenge. Their confidence suffers because they are faced with setbacks and they become self-critical when obstacles get in the way of their success.

To overcome being a Natural Genius, it's important to remind yourself that it's okay if you didn't hit the goal you set yourself. There is nothing wrong with you. Instead of bringing yourself down for not hitting the goal, be proud of how far along you have come to reach the place where you are.

Let's say you wanted to make $10,000 in one month but you only made $6,000. That is $6,000 more than $0, so that is still something to celebrate. You can figure out how you made that first $6,000 and replicate it to reach your goal.

Sometimes, what came easy a month ago might become difficult two months later. That's how life works. It's not always linear; it's more of a roller coaster. You have to remind yourself that some seasons in life will have challenges, and these challenges are what will build your strength and confidence.

Learn to practice positive self-talk. When you find yourself saying something bad about yourself, turn it around completely. This is what I do when I start to criticize myself. I have to catch myself all the time because I was in the habit of putting myself down if I made a mistake or I didn't reach my goal. Instead, I started to become my own best friend instead of my biggest critic.

The Soloist

The Soloist is the type of person who wants to do everything themselves. This person never wants to seek help because seeking help feels like an admission of weakness or like asking for a handout. But someone who thinks they have to do every single thing themselves can easily become overwhelmed, which leads to feeling inadequate and lonely.

Because the Soloist tends to feel like a failure when asking for help, they struggle to network with others in a social setting and are unable to accept constructive criticism.

As women, we frequently want to be a one-woman show in everything we do, but of course, trying to do everything yourself is actually counterproductive and leads to exhaustion and feeling like you are not enough. Women may be great at multitasking but by being a multitasker, you are actually unproductive. A report from mental health website Verywell Mind shows that while multitasking seems like it's a good thing, it can actually cause mental blocks, reducing comprehension and overall performance.[8]

To overcome this type of imposter syndrome, it's important to be okay with asking for help and knowing that you don't have to do everything yourself. I know that can be difficult, especially when you grew up in a culture teaching you that asking for help is a sign of weakness. Asking for help is a sign of strength, as is learning to accept that you don't have to do everything yourself.

Men rarely do this. If they don't know how to do a certain task, they just outsource it. I remember talking to a male colleague who wanted a virtual background for his Zoom account that would show his business logo. Instead of trying to figure out how to get this done himself (which is what most women would do, myself included), he just said he would hire someone do it for him.

Learn to be okay with asking for help. You don't have to be the one-woman show that society has told you to be. Not only is it *not* weak to ask for help, but doing so will boost your confidence a lot more when you look for and find the right kind of help.

The Expert

The Expert type means you are skilled or a specialist in a certain field, such as a doctor, a lawyer, or other professional, or someone with an advanced degree. As an Expert, you feel you should know everything in your specialized field because you have invested time and money in it, but a part of you still doubts your abilities to get the job done. The symptoms of an Expert are feeling the need to master every step in the process, feeling that you have to get more training and certifications, feeling like a fraud, and feeling so overwhelmed that you end up procrastinating.

I can totally relate to this because people look to me to help them learn about how to boost their confidence. I give talks and workshops on confidence and leadership for companies, universities, and other big organizations. Sometimes when an audience member asks me a question and I don't know that answer, I'm sure I have a shocked look on my face because I am supposed to know everything about confidence and leadership. This sends me down a rabbit hole of putting myself down. After all, I'm the "expert," so aren't I supposed to know the answer? If I don't, the person might think I'm stupid.

I finally realized that I don't have to know everything. If there's a question I can't answer, I can tell the person that I will personally get back to them with the information, or I can point them to a certain resource that will answer their question.

It's okay that you don't know everything even if you have an advanced degree or have studied a certain subject for many years. It's impossible to know every single thing. You are always learning something new. I have been talking about confidence and leadership for almost 10 years but to this day I am still learning new things. I know that I don't have the answers to every person's questions, and that is okay. It doesn't make me less of a person or less of an expert in my field.

One of the ways to overcome this issue is to reframe what it means to be an "expert." This really helped me in my journey. To be an expert, you just have to know a little bit more than your audience. By reframing what being an expert is, I learned to show up as the person I am today. And always be open to learning. I remember a teacher at school telling me that I will always be learning something new until the day I die. So you are never too young or too old to learn something new in your field.

Other ways to overcome this type of imposter syndrome is to show up as your authentic self. It's okay to be vulnerable and admit that you don't know everything. You are human, not a robot, and people can relate to you more when you share your vulnerabilities.

The Noticer

The Noticer is someone who always notices when something is not perfect, never celebrates their achievements, can't take compliments, and will always find something wrong even if everything went well. As a Noticer, you are okay with forgiving others if they make a mistake but cannot give yourself the same treatment.

I think this is something I can relate to, especially in my earlier days of forging my own path. I would always find something wrong in my work, which delayed my own success. I rarely shared any of my achievements because I didn't want to be boastful, and I was so fixated on noticing every wrong thing in what I was doing that I forgot to remember all the good things that I was able to achieve. It's easy to go down this route and feel like you are insufficient.

One way to overcome this is to practice loving yourself, embracing the good, the bad, and the ugly. For years, I would only love the good parts of me and hate the bad parts. But self-love means loving all of yourself, giving yourself grace, and becoming your own best friend. If your friend made a mistake, you wouldn't tell them they're a loser; you'd give them love and support. So why can't you do the same for yourself?

Practicing self-love is not easy, especially when you have to unlearn so many things that stopped you from loving yourself. My first book, *The Tao of Self-Confidence*, has a whole chapter on this topic that can help you start learning to love *all* of yourself and seeing how amazing you truly are.

The Discounter

The Discounter is a type of imposter syndrome that devalues your worth. You often find reasons to say that your achievements and your competence are not good enough or don't deserve recognition. You doubt yourself and your abilities. Also, you think that the skills and talents you possess are things everyone has.

I think being a Discounter is something that every woman can relate to because we have discounted our worth at least once in our lives. Have you ever discounted your prices in your business because you think you are not good enough or there's someone better out there? I have been guilty of that as well. It's important to know your worth and stop discounting it, so that others can see how amazing you can be.

I know this can be difficult, especially in a world where women still face so much unfairness. As a speaker, I deal with this all the time. You can charge your worth but there are people out there who don't see it and want to pay a fraction of your rate or even ask you to do it for free. And you willingly accept because you feel like you have no choice, but later you hear that a male speaker did the same exact job and got a much higher speaker rate. It's frustrating and demotivating when this happens.

How do we navigate this? It's important to speak up and learn to walk away when you feel like someone isn't valuing your worth. Even doing that can be hard because you may feel like you just walked away from the opportunity of your lifetime. There's no right or wrong answer, but I think the best thing to do is to listen to your intuition. We often ignore what our gut is telling us and end up in situations where we willingly discount our worth.

If you discount yourself, that is your default mindset, so one way to overcome this type of imposter syndrome is to change your mindset. This is very important because everything really starts with how you perceive yourself. One of the things I do is to listen to abundance mindset audios on YouTube for 30 minutes or more every morning to reprogram my brain. It can be tough sometimes when the world is so chaotic, but doing this has helped me increase my own sense of worth and even my income. Of course, listening to abundance audios doesn't mean money will fall from the sky, but it shows you that you are willing to take action in the things that you want to do to live a better life.

One more approach to overcoming the Discounter imposter syndrome is to embrace your strengths, skills, and talents. I am learning to do this as well. So many people tell me how amazing I am at marketing my book. To me it doesn't seem like a big deal because it's something that I do on a daily basis, so I don't tend to realize that most people cannot do what I do. I have to learn to stop discounting my own skills and learn to take ownership of it.

You may not even realize that the skills and talents you possess can be the ticket to creating a thriving business or getting the next promotion in your company. Lean into it and your future self will thank you for it. I hope that learning about these different types of imposter syndrome can help you figure out what type(s) you have and find ways to conquer them.

Overcoming Your Imposter Syndrome

If you are battling imposter syndrome right now, you are not alone. In fact, 70% of people have gone through imposter syndrome at some point in their lifetime.[9]

Knowing that you are not alone in experiencing imposter syndrome is important because we tend to feel like we have to go through these types of challenges on our own when actually the opposite is true. Whatever you're feeling, other people have felt it as well, including me. Fortunately, the business solutions company Asana has some common ways to overcome imposter syndrome.[10]

Focus on the Facts

One of the biggest reasons you have imposter syndrome is because you believe you are not good enough or you are not capable. Your brain picks up on these feelings and creates more stories to justify why you have imposter syndrome.

This is why it's important to separate your feelings from the facts. Just because you may feel a certain way doesn't mean it's your absolute truth. When you focus on the facts—the observable truths—it can prove that what you are feeling is not what's really going on.

Every time I have to speak in front of an audience, I have anxiety. What if I'm not good enough, or what if I give a bad talk? But when I do give my speech, the feedback I get from the audience is totally different from what I was feeling. People come up to me afterwards and tell me how I helped them see things from a different perspective, or how much they enjoyed listening to my talk. If I just decided to go with my feelings of imposter syndrome, I wouldn't be here today writing this book.

Acknowledge, Validate, Then Let Go

While it is important to focus on facts instead of feelings when it comes to imposter syndrome, it's just as important to know that those feelings do exist. Instead of ignoring them, learn to honor them, know that it's okay to feel those feelings, and then let them go so that you can show up as your best self.

One great way to do this is to journal. Every night before I go to bed, I write in my journal about what I was going through that day. Being able to write my feelings down makes me feel a lot better because I'm not repressing my feelings.

Share How You're Feeling

It can be a lonely road when you are going through imposter syndrome but it doesn't have to be that way. You can learn to share how you're feeling with someone you trust as a way to acknowledge and then let go of what you're going through. It's important to have that support system when you're going through imposter syndrome as a way to overcome it.

Talking to someone helps you find a new way to overcome your feeling of imposter syndrome. They always say two heads are better than one, so seek help when you need it. And if you need to seek a professional to overcome this, then do so. There is no shame in asking for help.

Look for Evidence

In moments of self-doubt, look for the evidence that you have achieved something of substance in your life. Consider your past achievements. If you have been able to conquer it once, you can conquer it again. If you were confident in one area of your life, you can transfer that same confidence in another area of your life.

Maybe you were able to run a full marathon, achieve your first $10,000 month, or land that promotion. That is proof of how capable you are.

One of the things I like to do is to create a "badass" list where I write down my past achievements. I go back to this list when imposter syndrome starts to creep up on me, and it helps me realize my own worth in the process and the successes I've had.

Reframe Your Thoughts

It's important to change the way you see things. Do you always have negative thoughts, which leads you to a feeling of imposter syndrome? Every time you think of something negative, it's important to think of the opposite so that you can get used to reframing your thoughts in a positive light. This takes some practice if you're not used to doing it, but in time it will become easier for you to switch your negative thoughts into positive ones.

When I feel insecure or like I'm not good enough, I really work on myself to see the positive instead of the negative. I concentrate on pushing those negative feelings away to make room for positive thoughts.

Look for a Mentor

Find a person you can learn from. A mentor looks different for everyone. Your mentor can be your closest friend, a coach you hired, or even just a book you like to read to help you get better. Remember, you don't have to overcome imposter syndrome by yourself. There are mentors out there who can show you the way to become better.

Toot Your Own Horn

It's important to acknowledge what you are good at and have the courage to celebrate your achievements. One thing I do when I'm feeling down is to check out the messages that people have sent me about how they loved reading my first book. These messages pump me up and remind me of the work I'm doing to help others become better. Instead of thinking I am not good, the messages remind me that I am capable of doing the work and doing it very well.

Now that we've done a deep dive on imposter syndrome, check out my podcast where I've interviewed over 800 women who share their journey to self-confidence (https://thetaoofselfconfidence .com). Hearing other women's struggles will help you feel less lonely and will also give you ideas to overcome what you are struggling with.

Now let's move on to talking about the gender confidence gap.

3

The Gender Confidence Gap

THE FIRST TIME I heard the term "gender confidence gap" was in 2020, when I was part of a group coaching program to learn how to become a better public speaker. It was always my dream to become a professional public speaker and to speak life into people, but I was too scared to go after it. This was the year I decided to go for it since we were all in lockdown and it was the best opportunity to learn.

One of the assignments was to give a 10-minute speech on any topic with no slides. As I was figuring out what I wanted to speak about for my assignment, I started searching the internet on different aspects of self-confidence that I could talk about.

For a couple of days, I was really focused on picking a topic that would give me joy to talk about. Then the words "gender confidence gap" popped up and I was intrigued. The more I read about it, the more I was convinced that this was the topic for my assignment. So I worked on my speech, which I titled "Eight Ways to Eliminate the Gender Confidence Gap."

For about a week, I practiced in front of the mirror. After I delivered my assignment, my coach told me the content was really good. It is now one of my main talks for corporations and organizations. Every time I speak about the gender confidence gap, the people organizing the event tell me how relevant this speech is because women continue to face this issue.

Unfortunately, many people are not yet familiar with the concept of the gender confidence gap. So we'll now explore what it is, the factors that create it, and how we have become socialized to it.

What Is the Gender Confidence Gap?

The Barnum Financial Group describes it this way:[1]

> The gender confidence gap refers to women generally feeling less confident in themselves and their abilities than men do, resulting in fewer chances at success in the workplace and beyond.

To expand on this, when men and women put themselves forward for a promotion, the woman will be 110% ready but something still holds her back from pursuing it, while the man will be about 30–50% ready but will just go for it. Even if men don't end up getting the promotion, they are okay that they went for it regardless of the outcome.

Now, I am not dissing the men. I think it's great that men believe they can figure it out as they go even if they have no clue where to start. Men just do things without overthinking them, and they often get results. Yet because of how they perceive themselves, women tend to think they are not good enough even when they truly have what it takes to go after a job or a promotion and thus will not even try. Men, on the other hand, take their chances and keep going until they get their desired outcome.

This is one of the reasons we see a gap in all industries between men and women in leadership roles. Of course, there are women who do move up through the ranks and have helped to open the doors for other women to be leaders in their own right. But it's only a small number compared to how many men take action. That's the gap.

Some key stats in a report from the data visualization platform Flourish help illustrate the gap between men and women today:[2]

- The global gender gap was 68% closed in 2023, which is a benchmark for the gender parity across 146 countries.
- Out of all regions, Europe has the highest gender parity at 76.3%, followed by North America (75%). The Middle East and North Africa (62.6%) are the regions the furthest away from parity.
- Gender parity will not be reached until the year 2154.
- In 2022, the parliaments in almost two out of three countries still had less than 30% women making up the whole body.
- As of February 2024, only 47 of the Fortune 500 companies were led by women.
- Female literacy rates are lower than the rates for males in most countries.
- Only 61% of women globally were employed or seeking employment in 2022—compared to 91% of men.

The fact that these numbers are still recent highlights the need for collective effort—both men and women must work together to uplift one another, foster confidence, and ensure more women pursue and attain leadership roles. This benefits not just individuals but organizations and society as a whole.

Factors That Contribute to the Gender Confidence Gap

So many factors affect the gender confidence gap. We're going to explore eight of them.

Men Get More Practice in Building Self-Confidence

Men have always received more practice than women when it comes to building self-confidence. A great example of this is dating. For many men, if they're hoping to get a woman's phone number, they may ask a large number of women and not be fazed by multiple rejections. Men are also raised to believe in themselves from a very young age, so their brains become wired to be okay with rejection and to learn to just go for it rather than fearing the potentially negative outcome. Men apply that concept in their careers too, and thus are more willing to go after that promotion than women are.

Women, on the other hand, are rarely taught to go after something they want and instead to take a passive attitude. Think of all the fairytales and romcoms where the woman has been programmed unconsciously to wait for Prince Charming to rescue her. Yet in real life, the only person who can save you is *you*!

Women Have Low Self-Confidence Due to Inaction

Inaction is one of the biggest reasons women deal with low self-confidence. Because most women feel they are not good enough, they don't even bother taking action, and that helps perpetuate their low self-confidence.

I understand, because I was the same way. For years I coasted through life and rarely took action in areas I wanted to succeed because I thought I wasn't good enough. I always assumed there was someone out there who was already doing what I was doing, so why bother. And the more I settled into inaction, the lower my self-confidence.

There are studies that show that women are more capable than they think when they finally do take action. American psychology researcher Dr. Zachary Estes, who studies the confidence of men and women, conducted an experiment to reorganize a 3D puzzle in a computer. When Estes checked out the results of men versus women, he saw that the men did better than the women. But what he also noticed was that the women did not even *attempt* to solve the puzzle. So Estes went back to the women and asked them to try again. The only requirement for the women was to *try* to solve the puzzle, regardless of the potential outcome. When the women did attempt to solve the puzzle, they scored the same as the men.[3]

Women Overthink More Than Men Do

Studies show that women tend to overthink things more than men do in almost all areas. I am guilty of this as well, and it delayed my own career trajectory for years because I thought I wasn't good enough or that I needed to do more to get everything "right." I would overthink to the point of inaction because I felt that something was still lacking. But really the only thing lacking was how I perceived myself: I still believed I was not worthy of going after what I truly wanted.

An article from the book summary platform Shortform discusses the ways that overthinking can really stunt a woman's self-confidence. Too much overthinking can lead to negative self-talk, dwelling on the past, losing focus on what's important, not finding effective solutions, and losing track of the big picture. The article also outlines the biological factors that make women overthink more than men:[4]

- Women tend to absorb more information than men, which causes overthinking.
- Women generally have a proportionally larger cingulate gyrus—the part of the brain that spots mistakes, considers options, and worries about things.
- Women have more brain matter than men in the prefrontal cortex and the limbic cortex. The prefrontal cortex is the part of the brain that we use for reasoning, while the limbic cortex is the part we use for processing emotions.
- In general, women's brains are more active than men's, which makes women more prone to overthinking than men do, and in turn can decrease their confidence.

This helps explain why there are so many thoughts running in my head at the same time, and why I have so many ideas for how to run my business but rarely execute at least one of those ideas. Are you guilty of that as well? I have spoken to so many women who have gone through the same thing. But knowing that biologically women overthink more than men shouldn't become an excuse for inaction. It's important to be aware of why we do this and then find ways to solve this problem.

The Glass Ceiling

The glass ceiling—that invisible barrier stopping women from moving into leadership roles—is a metaphor for the obstacles that prevent women and other marginalized people from attaining higher levels of professional success.

The glass ceiling was first coined by writer and consultant Marilyn Loden in 1978 at a panel discussion about women in the workplace. She was addressing the cultural challenges women face in moving up in their respective companies. The women were stuck in middle management and unable to advance.[5]

The concept of the glass ceiling does go beyond gender to include men of color and people in the LGBTQ+ community, for example. For the most part, the glass ceiling keeps women and others in marginalized groups from being promoted because they are considered less competent than white men even when they are more than capable of handling the job.

In an article in Psychology Today, Jaclyn Margolis and her research partner found that for every 100 men who get promoted to management roles, only 87 women get the same opportunity. They found that one of the biggest reasons why this still happens is because women end up doing more tasks at work that are not related to getting the promotion. In fact, a series of experiments found that women were almost 50% more likely to do the non-promotable tasks than men were since it was more expected for women to undertake these tasks than for men.[6]

The Broken Rung

Before shattering the glass ceiling, woman have to overcome another phenomenon: the "broken rung." Online education company Emeritus defines the broken rung as:[7]

a broken step on the corporate ladder, which becomes an obstacle that women face when trying to succeed in the corporate world. The concept suggests that women are unable to break through entry-level management roles and get promoted to higher levels, getting trapped in lower-level positions. The broken rung phenomenon results from systemic and cultural issues that pervade many workplaces. Despite the progress made toward gender equality, women continue to face challenges in ascending to leadership roles.

McKinsey's report "Women in the Workplace 2023" states the following about women in high-level corporate roles:[8]

- Women are still underrepresented in C-suite roles, representing only 28% of executives in 2023. This means that for every 100 C-suite occupants, only 28 are women, and six of those are women of color.
- The broken rung holds back Black and Latina women the most. For every 100 men who are promoted to manager, only 54 Black women are promoted and 76 Latinas.
- 78% of women who face microaggressions self-shield at work or adjust the way they look or act in an effort to protect themselves.

Companies need to do more to address the broken rung because it is a major reason why so many women, especially women of color, cannot move up the ladder. If women cannot even get their foot in the first round of corporate leadership, then everything above it is unattainable, thus denying women the chance to become the leaders they are meant to be.

Not Enough Positive Representation for Women

Representation is very important for women, especially those from marginalized cultures. Growing up in Toronto in the 1990s with hardly any Asian female role models to look up to made me feel small, and I thought I wasn't good enough to forge my own path. This is why it became my mission to help create the representation we deserve. At first I focused on Asian women because we have some of the lowest numbers of representation in leadership and media, but I also realized that in general women have less representation in every aspect compared to men.

So many women have been through hell but will never share their story because they think it doesn't matter. But it's actually very important to share your story with the world so other women can identify with it and learn from it. We must continue opening doors and forging paths to show other women what is possible, because how else can we keep moving forward?

An article in the *Guardian* pointed out that while the *Barbie* movie made waves by becoming the first movie directed by a woman to hit the billion-dollar mark, the number of female-led movies in Hollywood was at a 10-year low in 2023. Out of the 100 top-grossing films that year, only 30 featured a female lead and/or co-lead. The same article also notes:[9]

- In 2023, the number of films led by women of color fell from 18 to 14.
- Only three films in 2023 featured a woman over the age of 45 as a lead or co-lead, compared with 32 for men in the same age category.

A lack of positive representation can negatively affect a woman's confidence. Seeing is believing, so if you do not see someone who looks like you paving the way, you are less likely to pursue what you truly want to do. This is one of the reasons that it's important for women to show up and take up space in this world, to show both present and future generations what is possible.

If it wasn't for the few Asian women who have paved the way for me, I wouldn't be here today writing this book. At an event in Los Angeles I experienced one of the best moments of my life when I got to meet well-known journalist and TV personality Lisa Ling. I was able to talk to her, take photos with her, and even gift her a signed copy of my first book.

Lisa has been in the industry for over 30 years, and one of the reasons she became a journalist was that she saw another amazing Asian woman who was a journalist: Connie Chung. When I met Lisa, I thanked her for paving the way for me and for so many other women out there to dream bigger, because the right kind of representation can lead to a domino effect, creating more and more positive representation in any industry.

Positive representation is very important in helping to dismantle the negative stereotypes women still face today. By creating better representation, women can be seen as confident and courageous, instead of being stereotyped as the opposite. The more positive representation we have, the better.

Too Much Negative Representation for Women

The flip side of the lack of enough positive representation for women is the fact that we face so much negative representation that it can affect our mental health and confidence. How many times do women compare themselves to the perfectly edited photo of a supermodel on the cover of a fashion magazine, or to someone's carefully curated selfie on Instagram?

These unattainable images of beauty create many confidence issues for women. We are constantly reminded that we have to be a certain size, a certain skin color, and possess a certain type of beauty to feel good about ourselves.

Many studies emphasize the ways that unrealistic beauty standards can affect a woman's self-confidence and mental health. A report from the National Organization for Women highlights these statistics with regard to the body image and self-esteem of women and girls:[10]

- By age 13, 53% of American girls are "unhappy with their bodies." This rockets up to 78% by the time girls reach 17.
- 50% of teens are "self-conscious" about their bodies, and 26.2% report being "dissatisfied." By age 60, 28.7% of women feel "dissatisfied" and 32.6% feel "self-conscious" about their bodies.

- 45.5% of teens are considering cosmetic surgery; 43.7% of women over 60 are considering cosmetic surgery.
- When asked "Are you happy with your body?" 43.2% of teens and 37.7% of women in their 60s answered "yes."
- 40–60% of elementary-school-age girls are concerned about their weight or about becoming "too fat."
- A majority of girls (59%) reported dissatisfaction with their body shape, and 66% expressed the desire to lose weight.
- 46% of 9–11 year-olds are "sometimes" or "very often" on diets, and 82% of their families are "sometimes" or "very often" on diets.
- Studies conducted by Stanford University and the University of Massachusetts found that 70% of college women say they feel worse about their own looks after reading women's magazines.

These body-image issues also lead to eating disorders. The same National Organization for Women report also found the following:

- 15% of young women have substantially disordered eating attitudes and behaviors.
- Studies indicate that by their first year of college, 4.5–18% of women and 0.4% of men have a history of bulimia and as many as 1 in 100 females between the ages of 12 and 18 have anorexia.
- According to the Center for Mental Health Services, 90% of those who have eating disorders are women between the ages of 12 and 25.
- For females between 15 and 24 years old who suffer from anorexia nervosa, the mortality rate associated with the illness is 12 times higher than the death rate of all other causes of death.
- 20 million women and 10 million men suffer from a clinically significant eating disorder at some time in their life.
- The rate of development of new cases of eating disorders has been increasing since 1950.

All of this has an effect on a woman's confidence. When we become consumed with looking a certain way, there is no room to focus on the more important things. It doesn't help that some women of influence are obsessed with looking a certain way instead of showing up as their true self. We see countless photos on Instagram of perfectly edited bodies that can affect how we see ourselves.

During the 2024 Met Gala, as I was watching the celebrities with their amazing outfits, I noticed that Kim Kardashian showed up with a waist so small it appeared physically impossible. Many women want to achieve an hourglass shape, but Kim Kardashian took it so far that many women in the comments of her social media accounts were mad that she was portraying such an unattainable body image.

I have nothing against Kim Kardashian, but it's sad to see such a beautiful and smart woman be so consumed with how others think of her. Many times when she tries something new or extreme, it backfires, because she is trying too hard to be perfect when people are just craving authenticity. It doesn't help that the media tracks her every move, which puts even more pressure on her. I really did like her Met Gala dress but it would have been more effective without such a tightly cinched corset that gave her that impossibly small waist, which messed with her followers' perception of what it means to have the perfect body.

It's important to dismantle the many negative representations presented to women today. When we achieve more positive representation, we can create more women leaders in every industry.

Cultural Gender Confidence Gap

Most cultures favor men over women in most aspects of society, which in turn gives men more confidence to pursue what they want to do. As an Asian woman, I experienced this in my own family, where the men were always heavily favored over the women. My grandmother had to drop out of school in the sixth grade to help take care of her siblings, while her little brothers were the ones who went to school.

At that time, Chinese men were allowed to have more than one wife and even concubines to help have more heirs to carry the family name. Cultural upbringing can definitely hurt a woman's confidence, especially when you are told to hide in the background and never make any noise. It's harder for us to show up because our culture has told us to stay in our shell.

And it's not only Asian cultures that favor the men over women. According to Yahoo News, these are the worst countries for gender equality, as measured by the Gender Inequality Index and the Gender Development Index:[11]

1. Yemen
2. Nigeria
3. Somalia
4. Chad
5. Afghanistan
6. Liberia
7. Benin
8. Guinea-Bissau
9. Haiti
10. Sierra Leone
11. Côte d'Ivoire
12. Guinea
13. Niger
14. Mali
15. Democratic Republic of Congo
16. Papua New Guinea
17. Mauritania
18. Gambia
19. Malawi

20. Togo
21. Burkina Faso
22. Madagascar
23. Republic of Congo
24. Iraq
25. Cameroon

In some of these countries, women are married off before the age of 18, and most of the women live below the poverty line, have less education than men, do unpaid domestic work, are subjected to genital mutilation, have fewer women in leadership roles, and more.

How can women build confidence when they are treated this way and are not equipped with the right tools and resources?

Socialization

It's no surprise that men and women are accepted differently in society. How many times have women been told to get married and start a family because their "biological clock is ticking." Of course, there is nothing wrong with getting married and having children if that is something you desire. But society continues to make it seem like marriage is the ultimate goal for women, who are seen as little more than housewives and baby makers.

Football player Harrison Butker's 2024 commencement speech at Benedictine College, for example, was appalling. The fact that he told the female graduates that the most important role in their life would be a homemaker is terrible. While there is nothing wrong with choosing to be a homemaker, it is unacceptable to tell female graduates in the twenty-first century that they're better suited to marrying and running a household than pursuing a meaningful career. This is the part of the speech that enraged many people— both women and men:

For the ladies present today, congratulations on an amazing accomplishment. You should be proud of all that you have achieved to this point in your young lives. I want to speak directly to you briefly because I think it is you, the women, who have had the most diabolical lies told to you. How many of you are sitting here now about to cross this stage and are thinking about all the promotions and titles you are going to get in your career? Some of you may go on to lead successful careers in the world, but I would venture to guess that the majority of you are most excited about your marriage and the children you will bring into this world.

I can tell you that my beautiful wife, Isabelle, would be the first to say that her life truly started when she began living her vocation as a wife and as a mother. I'm on the stage today and able to be the man I am because I have a wife who leans into her vocation. I'm beyond blessed with the many talents God has given me, but it cannot be overstated that all of my success is made possible because a girl I met in band class back in middle school would convert to the faith, become my wife, and embrace one of the most important titles of all: homemaker.[12]

It's diabolical lies like the ones Butker told in his speech that can hinder a woman's confidence and convince her this is all she is good for and nothing more. The impact of that means there are fewer women in leadership roles, fewer women paving the way and showing current and future generations their limitless possibilities.

And there is also the issue of how much money these women spent on getting their education. Per the website for Benedictine College, the tuition for the 2024–2025 school year tuition is $35,350.[13] And this is just tuition; it doesn't include room and board, textbooks, or other expenses. So, after spending more than $140,000 over four years for tuition alone to get a college degree, female graduates were being told to become homemakers instead of applying their knowledge and ideas to starting a business or join the corporate ladder. It's beyond insulting.

Many people were appalled by Butker's speech. Even the nuns from Benedictine College disagreed and shared the following statement:[14]

> The sisters of Mount St. Scholastica do not believe that Harrison Butker's comments in his 2024 Benedictine College commencement address represent the Catholic, Benedictine, liberal arts college that our founders envisioned and in which we have been so invested. *[This is just the beginning of the statement; you can read the full statement on their Facebook page.[15]]*

It's important for women to stop believing the diabolical lies that toxic men tell them. If women are constantly told to behave a certain way, how can they gain the confidence to pursue their dreams or become the leaders they are meant to be?

Industries Strongly Affected by the Gender Confidence Gap

The gender confidence gap affects nearly every industry. I want to talk about three segments in particular: STEM, entrepreneurship, and the entertainment industry.

Gender Confidence Gap in STEM

It's no secret that there is a huge gap in the numbers of men and women working in STEM (science, technology, engineering, math). The Institute of Engineering and Technology notes that while there are over one million women in STEM occupations, this only accounts for 29% of the STEM workforce.[16]

What are some of the factors that can affect these numbers? Adina Sterling, a professor from Stanford Graduate School of Business, conducted a study with recent college graduates on why there is a confidence gap between men and women in STEM. Her findings include:[17]

- When she asked students with engineering degrees to rank their performance level and self-efficacy levels, she noticed that the female graduates had lower levels of self-efficacy than the male graduates.
- Women who enter the workforce make less money than their male colleagues; this results in less confidence to carry out their technical tasks.
- The study also revealed that the salary gap between men and women in STEM is because women tend to rank themselves lower when it comes to self-efficacy, which is the main thing that employers are looking for. If a woman doesn't have the confidence for the job, the employer will either give her less pay than her male colleague or might not hire her at all.
- Women make less than $61,000 in entry-level STEM roles, while men make $65,000 or more, which contributes to the gender confidence gap.
- Self-promotion also plays in a key role between men and women. Women are less likely to promote themselves, which can hinder the progress of having more women in the STEM workforce.

Of course, women still face gender biases in STEM but it is also up to us to know our worth, start showing up, and start showing the world that we are capable of getting the job done. If women continue to lower their worth, it will take longer to close the gender gap in STEM and will perpetuate the inequalities for all women who want to enter the STEM workforce.

Gender Confidence Gap in Entrepreneurship

The world of entrepreneurship is still very much dominated by men. While the numbers of women in entrepreneurship are growing in the United States, women still face many situations that keep them from realizing their full potential. Here are some stats about women entrepreneurship from Clarify Capital, as of 2024:[18]

- Currently, women wield approximately $10 trillion in financial assets within the U.S. This number is expected to surge to $30 trillion by the close of the decade.
- Women-led companies generated approximately $1.9 trillion in earnings, employed 10.9 million people, and maintained an annual payroll of $432.1 billion.
- The primary sectors for women-owned businesses include retail (26%), health, beauty, and fitness services (17%), and food and restaurants (14%).
- Women-owned companies rose 16.7% between 2012 and 2019, compared to 5.2% for men-owned businesses.
- Over the last 20 years, there has been a 114% growth in the number of women-owned firms in the United States.

So it seems like women entrepreneurs are doing a great job—and they are!—and yes, women have made so much progress. But here's some other facts about women entrepreneurship from the same article that shows just how much they lag behind their male counterparts:

- A significant 59% of women business owners acknowledge having to exert more effort to achieve the same level of success as their male counterparts.
- As of 2022, U.S. female founders receive only 2.1% of venture capital funding.
- Roughly 53% of businesses owned by women are financed through personal savings, while 15% of women-owned businesses are financed through private business loans.
- On average, female business owners anticipate attaining equitable access to capital by the year 2031.
- Men are two times more likely to gain more than $100,000 in funding than women.

- Among the 33.2 million small businesses in the United States, approximately 13 million are owned by women.
- Out of the total entrepreneur population, 41.5% are women, while 58.5% are men.

It's quite alarming that a large number of women must self-fund their businesses. I have spoken to so many women who have used most of their savings to get the ball rolling. The fact that men are twice as likely to get $100,000 more funding than women is terrible.

These statistics underline the notion that women aren't capable of running a business, even though that is far from the truth. And because women are more likely to get turned down for funding, it can also hinder their confidence. This is one of the reasons that women represent only 2.1% of the funding in the VC world, and of course the statistics for women of color are even bleaker. And women have to work much harder than men to prove that they are worth being funded.

Another thing that women must contend with are the so-called male "gurus" who tell their audience that they have to hustle 24 hours a day to make their business successful. Men have much more time to devote to their business, while many women are forced by circumstances to think about their children, other family members, household errands, and more. Most men have the luxury to "hustle" in their business because they don't have to worry about prepping lunches, picking up the kids, shopping for groceries, and all the other mundane, time-consuming tasks that women deal with every day.

Running a household is a full-time job on its own. If it wasn't for these male gurus' wives running the household in the background, they wouldn't be as successful as they are today. They usually take the credit without acknowledging that there's a woman behind the scenes making sure that everything doesn't fall apart. I know this because my great-grandfather ran a successful shipping business that is still run today by his sons. His business wouldn't have thrived as it did if it wasn't for my great-grandmother, who had to run the household and hold down the fort. They had to make it work as a team. My great-grandmother raised 12 kids plus cared for in-laws and grandchildren—no easy task. I have to commend my great-grandmother for what she did because she is part of my great-grandfather's success and legacy.

This kind of talk from the male gurus can make women feel bad for not working on their business 24/7. You may feel like a failure because you can't be like the bros who can work on their business constantly with no other responsibilities. But give yourself some grace and be okay with what you can do because you do so much already.

With all the additional opportunities that men get to win in entrepreneurship compared to women, it's not surprising that women have less confidence in their entrepreneurship abilities than men do. A report from the marketing platform AI Bees shared some discouraging stats comparing men and women when it comes to entrepreneurship:[19]

- 64% of female entrepreneurs raised less than $10,000 for their business venture, compared to 14% of male entrepreneurs.
- 40% of men begin their entrepreneurial journey before the age of 35 versus 33% of women.
- 8% of men begin their entrepreneurial journey before the age of 25 versus 3% of women.
- 56% of men spend half of their day working compared to 43% of women.
- Men are 72.4% more confident in their ability to succeed, compared to women, who are 65.3% sure.

When you see these facts, it's no wonder women still have a confidence gap in entrepreneurship. Other contributing factors are that women tend to overthink more and delay starting because they want everything to be perfect. Men are more willing to start, make mistakes, and figure it out along the way. I was one of those people who wanted everything to be 100% perfect and thought everyone else had it all figured out, and because of that, I delayed my own success.

Also, men and women's intentions for starting a business may be totally different. Women often want to make a little extra money or just have more freedom for themselves, and men tend to be more intentional when it comes to starting a business. Men target the right audience to make a profit and eventually sell the company. Women are rarely taught about having an "exit strategy" for their business.

It's no wonder that women still face a huge confidence gap compared to men in entrepreneurship, but it's also up to us to change these statistics. Right now, women are still underrepresented in the field, but we can change the numbers. The more women in entrepreneurship, the more we can grow our confidence from it as well.

The Entertainment Industry

It's no secret that women have been preyed upon in Hollywood and elsewhere in the industry for decades, and despite more awareness nowadays it is still ongoing. Diddy was in the center of this news in 2024 when a video was leaked to CNN showing the music mogul physically assaulting his then-girlfriend Cassie Ventura in the hallway of a Los Angeles hotel in 2016. I wish I could unsee that appalling video of that predator stomping on an innocent woman, dragging her across the floor, and even throwing things at her.[20]

Most women are too afraid to speak up when things like this happen because of the powerful men who rule the entertainment industry. Diddy faces multiple accusations of sexual abuse from women as young as 17 years, but he's not the only person who has preyed on innocent women by promising them fame and fortune in exchange for personal favors. I talked about Harvey Weinstein earlier in the book. It's no wonder women have gone through so much trauma in their careers feeling like they have no one to talk to about this, much less reporting anything to the authorities.

I commend Cassie for having the courage to file a lawsuit against Diddy. It's not easy for victims of sexual or domestic violence to come forward, especially when there are powerful players involved. These predators have gatekeepers who protect them from the law and can literally get away with murder. Cassie and her legal team would have had to make sure they had all the available evidence before filing, which can take years of planning in the hopes that the person responsible will be punished.

As a result of the video being leaked to CNN, Cassie was able to speak out for the first time, and her statement is important. According to an article in *Variety*, here is what she posted on her Instagram account:[21]

Thank you for all of the love and support from my family, friends, strangers and those I have yet to meet," Cassie wrote. "The outpouring of love has created a place for my younger self to settle and feel safe now, but this is only the beginning. Domestic Violence is THE issue. It broke me down to someone I never thought I would become. With a lot of hard work, I am better today, but I will always be recovering from my past.

Thank you to everyone that has taken the time to take this matter seriously. My only ask is that EVERYONE open your heart to believing victims the first time. It takes a lot of heart to tell the truth out of a situation that you were powerless in.

I offer my hand to those that are still living in fear. Reach out to your people, don't cut them off. No one should carry this weight alone.

This healing journey is never ending, but this support means everything to me. Thank you.

Cassie is right; imagine how many women who are victims of domestic violence are too afraid to share their story whether they are in Hollywood or not. The victims instead get blamed for not leaving the relationship sooner or for not speaking up sooner, being told they are responsible. As you are reading this book, there is a woman out there right now who is being assaulted by a man and she doesn't have the platform to tell her truth. So please, let's support the real victims of domestic abuse and be on their side.

Here's some facts about domestic violence from National Coalition Against Domestic Violence:[22]

- On average, nearly 20 people per minute are physically abused by an intimate partner in the United States. Over the course of one year, this equates to more than 10 million women and men.
- 1 in 7 women and 1 in 25 men have been injured by an intimate partner.
- Women between the ages of 18 and 24 are most commonly abused by an intimate partner.
- Domestic victimization is correlated with a higher rate of depression and suicidal behavior.
- 1 in 5 women and 1 in 71 men in the United States has been raped.

And this type of behavior has been going on for decades. An article from the History Channel explains the Hollywood Dictatorship, where the men were able to do what they wanted without any consequences. There would be so called "stag parties" where innocent women were invited to the party only to be sexually assaulted by the men in attendance. Some of the women who were raped at these parties were as young as 17. Back in the 1930s, there was no such things as the #MeToo Movement or sexual harassment cases. Women were just expected to be available for powerful men at any given moment. And these women were left with so much unresolved trauma because even when they tried to tell someone, Hollywood executives would just find ways to dismiss their story. And they paid doctors to ensure there was no evidence of rape or other assault.[23]

Often the innocent victim gets blamed for the incident and must carry that unnecessary shame with her. When Cassie filed her lawsuit against Diddy, many people accused her of lying about the whole thing and only changed their tune after the video was leaked. So of course in this kind of climate, men are more confident than women in the industry, especially when they think the men are untouchable, like Diddy.

And because women cannot advance as fast as men in Hollywood, there are fewer women represented in the film industry, in the studios, both in front of and behind the cameras. The World Economic Forum notes that since 1929, only 17% of Oscar nominees have been women, and less than 2% were women of color. Only 16% of Oscar winners have been women.

The gender confidence gap has certainly affected women in a negative way and in many industries. It's important to close the gap so that more women are placed in leadership roles and achieve gender parity at a faster rate, because 130 years is much too long to wait for gender parity to be achieved.

After reading this chapter, the most important thing you can do is work on your mindset. You'll find some free resources at https://taoqueens.com/gift to work on developing that mindset to overcome the gender confidence gap. Another way we can achieve gender parity is to help women develop courage so that they can build the confidence to be the leader they are meant to be. This is the focus of the next chapter.

4

Courage Before Confidence

I USED TO think that you needed confidence to have courage and I was wrong. The truth is that courage comes first. You have to build up your courage and, in turn, you start to build your confidence. It's your courage that will propel you to take action and seize the opportunities that come your way. Developing courage isn't easy but it's needed for gaining that oh-so-important confidence.

This chapter is all about courage and how you can develop it so you can have the confidence to be the leader you are meant to be.

Definition of Courage

First and foremost, it's important to understand the definition of courage. Various dictionaries offer similar definitions, but the description I like best is one I found in an article in *Psychology Today* that paraphrases Stanley Rachman's view of courage from his book *Fear and Courage:*[1]

> Courage is the quality of mind or spirit that enables a person to face difficulty, danger, pain, etc. despite anxiety or fear. That is,

if one does not experience anxiety or fear about doing something then it is easy to do and does not require courage or strength.

I always tell people in my talks that to be fearless doesn't mean you have no fear. Being fearless is about feeling the fear and doing it anyway. It takes a lot out of us to push through our fears and this is where courage comes into play, because once you conquer that fear, you start to build the confidence to tackle the next thing.

It really starts with your mind and knowing you have what it takes even if you have fears or anxiety. To this day, when I go into a talk, I still have fear and anxiety because I always want to do my best. I want to make sure that the audience will walk away with something that can help them take at least one more step forward toward their greatness.

With courage you can build your confidence, and that is how you stop playing small and take on the big plans in your life. This book will be with you in every step of the way. Here's some ways you can start building courage today in your career and life.

Acknowledge Your Fear

The first and most important thing you must learn to do in developing courage is to acknowledge that your fears do exist. Every single person in this world experiences some type of fear. Ignoring the fears you need to conquer will just delay you from the life you are meant to live.

There are reasons why we experience fears. It can be because of past traumas, our upbringing, our environment, and more. It can be as simple as fear of the unknown. Remember that as children, we started out fearing nothing. When we are young, we have the courage to start walking, climb ladders, jump from couch to couch because we think we are superheroes. But as we grow older, we start to learn new things, and for the first time we start to experience what we fear, or what others told us to fear, and it stops us from doing the things we loved doing as children. As we grow older, more fears start to creep in, and if we continue to ignore them they will hold us back from stepping into our greatness.

Having fears isn't a bad thing. Fear can be a sign that we are ready to take ourselves to the next level. It tests our strength and resilience, which builds our courage and confidence.

There are so many acronyms for FEAR, but my favorite is one that I heard from a speaker over 10 years ago:

False

Evidence

Appearing

Real

I try to remind myself of this acronym when I start to feel scared about taking the next step in my goal or journey. I take a step back and ask myself why I am feeling this way. You may not realize this but your brain is also trying to protect you from what happened to you in the past. It has good intentions but it's also not allowing you to grow.

I remember coaching a woman who was afraid to attend parties because she was afraid to talk to groups of people. It got to the point that she couldn't even say her name in a group setting. I asked her why she was afraid. At first, she didn't say anything. She put up a wall, thinking I was attacking her when in reality I wanted to know the root cause of why she felt this way.

I told her that for me to help her, she needed to be open and honest with me if she truly wanted to overcome this fear. Finally, she told me that 10 years earlier, she went to a concert with a bunch of friends and the group decided to leave her. She ended up being alone at the concert. Because of that, her brain was trying to protect her from being in this situation again.

I told the woman that what happened 10 years ago was not the same situation as now. Her friend invited her to the party, which meant her presence was wanted. The people there would not be the same group of people who left her at the concert. The people at the party would want to talk to her and get to know her. After that session, she attended the party and her fear of talking to people in a group setting went away.

If you want to learn a great way to get to the root cause of your fears, I like the Five Whys technique. It was invented in the 1930s by Sakichi Toyoda, the founder of Toyota Industries, and Toyota still uses the Five Whys today. The purpose of the technique is super simple: when you encounter a problem, you find the root cause by asking why five times. By the fifth time, you have figured out the root cause and you can start finding ways to solve or overcome the problem.[2]

Here's a great example that I used in my own journey:

My fear: I am afraid to write my first book.

Why? I know nothing about leadership.

Why? I suck at grammar.

Why? I think there are people who have more knowledge than me about leadership.

Why? I've never written a book all by myself.

Why? I don't think I am the right candidate for this opportunity.

I thought the real reason why I was afraid to write my first book was because I had no knowledge about leadership. But by diving deeper through each why, I saw that the real reason was because I didn't think I was good enough for the job. It took the encouragement of others telling me that I have what it takes to write the book. As a result, I committed myself to writing the book even if I still felt like I wasn't good enough. Knowing that I had other people rooting for me and believing in me helped me make the decision to go for it. I'm glad I was able to get out of my own way to write the first book, which in turn gave me the confidence to write this book.

I hope that this technique can help you get to the root cause of your fears so that you can find ways to overcome them.

Positive Self-Talk

What you say to yourself matters. If you are constantly putting yourself down, you won't build the courage you need to take action on the things you truly want to do. This is why it's important to change the way you talk to yourself for the better.

One thing that really helps me practice positive self-talk is by listening to positive audio. If you are unable to talk to yourself in a positive light, then you can find audio that will do the positive self-talk for you. There are many audios on YouTube available for this. It's also impactful to hear positive talk from someone you look up to because you are more likely to take it seriously.

Keep in mind that practicing positive self-talk doesn't mean that you have to be positive 100% of the time. That's unattainable because the nature of life is that you will encounter days when you are less positive. I had to learn that the hard way. I thought I always had to be positive all the time to the point where I started crying in my room for no reason. I didn't realize there was such a thing as toxic positivity.

Yes, it is important to have a positive mindset but it's important and okay to feel your feelings when times are tough. Just remember, "It's okay not to be okay." You don't want to repress those feelings as well.

The purpose of practicing positive self-talk is to help you train your brain to take action on the things that are holding you back. Have you been procrastinating on a task or you are too afraid to take your first step in creating your new path? This is where you utilize positive self-talk to get it done.

Alina Health outlines a number of effective ways of practicing positive self-talk:[3]

- *Think about your thinking.* If you are experiencing negative thoughts, try to slow it down instead of letting it pass by. Write it down or question yourself why you are feeling this way. Practicing this can help you get to the root cause of the negative thoughts, and then you can start finding ways to correct it.
- *Challenge your negative beliefs.* Learn to ask the right questions when negative thoughts appear. By asking the right questions, you can start seeking the right answers and prove your negative thoughts wrong.
- *It's got to be believable.* Do your best to replace your negative thoughts with more balanced and evidence-based thoughts. Just having a generalized positive thought will not make you feel better. Instead, it feels like an empty promise. Balanced and evidence-based thoughts help you practice positive self-talk step by step.
- *Repeated practice.* Practice makes progress, so trying it once won't work. It has to become a habit. Yes, in the beginning it will feel awkward and weird. The more you practice, the better you will get at it.
- *Stay in the present.* Bringing up past negative experiences and worrying about the future will not do you any good. This is why it's important to stay focused and in the present.
- *Laugh.* Laughter is the best medicine, right? Sometimes a good laugh can go a long way as long as it doesn't hurt others. You can laugh by yourself or share the moment with your friends.

Identify Your Strengths

Being a woman isn't easy when you feel like you have to do everything yourself because society told you that you are "Superwoman." But it's important to know what your strengths are so you can focus on them.

You have been good at some things at different points in your life, correct? One of the things I have done was to create a badass list of the things that I have accomplished that I can always turn to when I have bad days. Creating a badass list will give you the motivation to work on yourself and your courage. If you have been successful at something, remember the things you did to make that happen and see if you can transfer what you did to future situations.

By focusing and working on your strengths, you are more likely to:

- Take action
- Be happier
- Increase your confidence and courage
- Be less depressed
- Have greater resilience

But what if you don't even know what your strengths are? No worries, there are many ways to find out your strengths. One way to start identifying your strengths is to take a strengths test, and you can find many strengths tests online. A popular one that many executives take is the CliftonStrengths created by Gallup. There is a fee to take it but it does give you a very detailed assessment at the end. Doing a test like this can help you focus on what you are good at and start taking action.

Another way you can identify your strengths is to ask your family and friends to write down what they think your strengths are. There are also various support systems, tools, and resources that can help you identify your strengths, such as character strength worksheets, reading books on this topic, or attending workshops related to identifying your strengths.

Practice Makes Progress

It's important to practice having courage. In the beginning, it will feel uncomfortable and awkward because it's something new to you.

But the more you keep practicing it, the more comfortable it will feel and the better you become at it.

How do you practice courage? Start small. Find small acts of courage that you are able to tackle. It can be as simple as wearing a new color in your wardrobe or learning a new hobby. Learning to be brave doesn't require a big gesture.

One of the biggest (small) ways I was able to build courage was learning to be on video. This really scared me so I delayed doing it so many times before I finally decided to press the record button. The first time I recorded myself on video, it was a hot mess. It took me two hours to record a two-minute video. But I did it. The more I kept recording videos of myself, the better I became at being on camera and that fear started to go away.

Being able to practice courage every day allows you to be prepared for the moments in your life that you cannot control, like the pandemic. That was a huge change for everyone and the ones who came out of it winning were the people who knew how to find ways to overcome this fear of the unknown and had the courage to pivot their businesses or even to start new business ventures.

It's Okay to Fail

Failure is not easy, especially when you are told that failure is bad for you. In fact, it's the total opposite. Failure is a great way to help you build your courage because life can be tough and failure teaches you to pick yourself back up in any situation, learn from your mistakes, and find solutions to move forward. There will be times in your life where the actions you take will make you question your path. It also doesn't help that people rarely share their failures.

The most successful people in the world have gone through many failures en route to getting to where they are today. I think knowing the failures endured by successful people can help you realize that you are not alone in this journey. I also have had my fair share of failures over the years from the time I failed kindergarten for coloring outside the lines of my photo to failing in parts of my entrepreneurial journey.

Here are some famous accomplished women who failed before they found huge success in their careers.[4]

Simone Biles

Simone Biles is considered the greatest gymnast of all time. Yet in 2011 she didn't make the U.S. women's junior national team. This didn't stop Biles, however. In fact, she started training harder so that she could be part of the team, and in 2012 she went on to finish third in the U.S. junior all-around competition. Then she won her first U.S. senior all-around in 2013, and since then has the most gold medals of any gymnast in history and was awarded the Presidential Medal of Freedom in 2022.

Sha'Carri Richardson

Sha'Carri Richardson became the fastest woman in the world in 2023 when she won the women's 100 meter at the Track and Field World Championships. Before Richardson made history, she was given a 30-day suspension for cannabis use. Her win in 2020 was invalidated, and she was not allowed to compete in the 2021 Tokyo Olympics. Then she failed to qualify for the 2022 World Athletics Championships. Instead of quitting, Richardson kept on competing and eventually beat the late Florence Griffith Joyner's 35-year-old record for the 100-meter dash.

JK Rowling

JK Rowling made a name for herself with the *Harry Potter* franchise. Her book series is now a household name with movies, toys, clothes, stage shows, and a theme park experience. Her journey started with rejections from 12 publishers for her synopsis of Harry Potter.

One of the things JK Rowling has done was share her first rejection letter on social media to inspire others not to give up and to remind them that rejection is part of the process.

Beyoncé

We now know that everything Beyoncé touches turns to gold. Her concerts sell out in minutes and anything tied to her name sells out right away. She is called Queen Bey for a reason. But before all of this, Beyoncé experienced failure as a child when she was in a girl group called Girl's Tyme. Their group competed on *Star Search* in 1993 and lost to a rock band. That didn't stop Beyoncé from becoming a superstar. She went on to become part of Destiny's Child, which became a huge success, and today she is one of the most successful solo artists ever, winning multiple Grammy Awards and other accolades. Beyoncé even plays a clip of her time on *Star Search* in her video for "Flawless" as a way of acknowledging her failures.

Katy Perry

Katy Perry is a successful musician with hit songs like "California Girls" and "Firework." Before that, her very first album was a gospel album called *Katy Hudson* and it only sold 200 copies, a considerable commercial flop. This never stopped Katy Perry from her musical journey. In 2019, she was the world's highest-paid woman in music and also became a judge on *American Idol*. I never even knew Katy Perry released a gospel album, and it's good to know that just because you fail at one genre of music, doesn't mean you fail at others.

Oprah Winfrey

Everyone knows who Oprah is. She has built one of the most successful media companies in the world and is the richest African

American woman in the world. Even though Oprah has made quite a name for herself, she has had her fair share of failures to go along with it. In 1988, she produced and starred in her first big-budget movie, *Beloved*, and the movie tanked at the box office. Instead of quitting, Oprah learned a valuable lesson from it. She told *Vogue*, "It taught me to never again—never again, ever—put all of your hopes, expectations, eggs in the basket of [the] box office. Do the work as an offering, and then, whatever happens, happens." Oprah followed her own advice, of course, and has expanded into creating her own TV network, investing in real estate, and more.

Vera Wang

Vera Wang is one of the most famous fashion designers in the world, with people fighting to wear her unique pieces while walking down the aisle. Yet her journey didn't start out as a success. In fact, she began as a figure skater but didn't qualify for the Olympics in 1968. Wang went on to work for *Vogue* as an assistant and became a fashion editor within a year. When she was denied the editor-in-chief position at *Vogue*, she decided to start her own fashion line at the age of 40. I always say that when one door closes, another one opens, and Vera Wang is a great example of that.[5]

These women are successful because their failures taught them to be courageous enough to turn their dreams into reality. It wasn't an easy thing to do but it was definitely worth going through the failures to become the powerhouse women they are today. If these women can fail and then succeed, you can too.

Celebrate Your Courageous Acts

It's important to celebrate every single courageous act you have done in your life. Most people think that you can only celebrate when you finally make it big, but really it can be in every moment of your life.

Think about all the times you had to be courageous enough to take a leap of faith into your journey. It takes guts to get out there and make it happen, even more so when you get rejected time and time again but you still keep going. You must celebrate your perseverance as much as possible because it's these moments in life that will get you to the big moment you've been waiting for.

The small moments are important to celebrate, and this is how you continue to build your courage step by step, bit by bit. The small, actionable daily steps will help yield the massive results you are looking for.

One thing you can do is create a list of courageous acts that you want to celebrate and figure out how you will celebrate them. You can reward yourself with some down time or buy something nice for yourself. Whatever it is that is meaningful to you, get into the habit of celebrating the courageous acts you achieve in your life because *you* made it happen, regardless of the mistakes made along the way. You got there and it's worth celebrating!

It's Okay to Ask for and Receive Help

It's important to remind yourself that it's really okay to ask for help when you need it. This is not the time to think that, as a woman, you have to do everything yourself. I know how hard it can be to ask for help because we have been told we are weak if we do. And it's also okay to receive help when people offer it to you.

If you don't like to ask for or receive help, you are not the only one. I used to hate it as well. I still get uncomfortable when people ask me what I need support with. My anxiety level creeps up, and I start thinking to myself that it's shameful for me to take help from others.

I am part of a women's cohort that holds a 90-minute mentoring session month where we talk about our goals and what we are going through in our life, whether business or personal. Toward the end of one particular mentoring circle, one of the co-chairs told us to type in the Zoom chat what we needed help with. I wondered whether or not I should share what I needed help with. There were about two minutes left before the session ended. I was still contemplating if I should do it or not. In my head, I was saying to myself, "What if people think I am no good because I am asking for help? What if I am seen as a fraud because the person who is an expert on confidence and leadership is asking for help? People are going to think I am weak because I'm sharing what I need help with."

And finally, just before the session ended, I typed in the Zoom chat what I needed help with. A couple of days later, the co-chair who had us state what we needed help with reached out to me and said she was going to help me with my request. That day, I realized that receiving help is just as important as asking for help.

It's still taking me a while to reframe how I see help and unlearn the things I was taught. In my culture, asking for help is considered a sign of weakness or an indication that you are asking for a handout. Because of this perception, I hated getting help from anybody. My pride got the best of me, which ended up delaying my own success. I realize now how my pride was stopping me from my own greatness and I had to learn to say yes when people offered to help.

Don't get me wrong, to this day I still get very uncomfortable when people ask me how they can support me. It's a learning process, but you would be surprised by some of the outcomes, as I have been. Give yourself permission to receive help from others who want the best for you. This will help build your courage along the way, and it's better when you can do this with the support of other people.

I hope all this can be the starting point for you to develop your courage because it's so necessary to have that foundation for building your confidence. It will not be easy or pretty, but your future self will thank you for it.

After reading this chapter, it's important to start practicing courage, even if it takes you just one step forward. You can use the strategies mentioned in this chapter as a start. I believe that creating the small actionable daily steps is what will yield big results.

Now if you really want to practice courage as a woman, the best way to do that is to learn how to self-promote. I know what you are thinking: I hate self-promotion!

Don't worry, I'm not a big fan of it either, but it really helped me build my courage to put myself out there and learn to be unapologetically myself. There are so many benefits you receive when you promote yourself. So let's get to the next chapter so you can start putting your courage skills to the test.

5

Why Self-Promotion Empowers Women

SELF-PROMOTION IS SOMETHING I thought I would never do. The first time I decided to start a blog, I wrote a whole paragraph but was too scared to share it because I was afraid of what people might think of me—afraid that my peers would laugh at me. I did share it on Facebook, but only on a private setting, so it didn't reach many people.

Over the years, I would share a couple of things here and there, still a little bit scared and uncomfortable doing so because I was always told that promoting yourself isn't "ladylike," And because I am an Asian woman, my culture taught me it's improper to share my achievements because it's bragging.

It wasn't until I was part of *Asian Women Who BossUp* that I realized the power of self-promotion and where it could lead me. Every time I shared the book on social media or through someone's private message, I was asked to speak to corporations, which led to other opportunities. That was when I decided to promote myself, even though it still felt scary and uncomfortable, because I wanted to normalize it for women—and for myself.

And yes, of course, some people tell me I share too much or promote the same thing too many times. I share it anyway because there are people watching what you do even when you are not aware of it. Many women send me messages that my showing up gives them the permission to show up themselves.

So I made a decision to show up, not just for myself but to demonstrate to all women that self-promotion isn't tacky, or bragging, or distasteful at all. I want them to realize that self-promotion is actually empowering.

My favorite example is the *Barbie* movie. During the summer of 2023, you couldn't go anywhere without seeing the color pink. Mattel collaborated with a wide variety of companies to sell Barbie-themed merchandise—luggage, clothes, home decor, and much more, even a Barbie-themed Xbox!

The promotion was relentless, and *Barbie* became the first billion-dollar movie directed solely by a woman. It reached that milestone just 17 days from the movie's release date. This is a big deal because for decades, Hollywood decreed that women-centered movies are not as profitable as movies centering men (despite evidence to the contrary) and *Barbie* proved them wrong (again). *Barbie* was also the fastest Warner Bros. movie to hit one billion dollars.[1]

This is a prime example of why self-promotion is important for women. It breaks barriers and opens the door for women to see what is possible for themselves. By hiding your skills and talents you are doing a disservice to yourself and to the world.

This chapter will help you realize the importance and the power of self-promotion, both for yourself and for current and future generations of women.

Factors Discouraging Women from Self-Promotion

It's important to understand the circumstances of the various factors that hinder women from self-promotion. Bringing awareness to them can help us overcome them, and can help bridge the gender confidence gap we still face today.

Self-Promotion Is Not "Ladylike"

From the moment they're born, women are programmed to believe that self-promotion is not ladylike or is distasteful for women to do. Culturally, women are generally told not to be boastful or to brag. But why is it okay for men to share their achievements and not women? Who decided that self-promotion for women is not acceptable? This myth hurts all women because it stops us from sharing our gifts and achievements with the world.

"Ladylike" means that women are expected to be polite and demure, to act and behave a certain way that society considers "appropriate." I fell into the trap of thinking that sharing your own products or services is not ladylike. But if you're an entrepreneur, how are you supposed to make a living if you don't promote yourself?

It's important to stop thinking that self-promotion is not ladylike. The more women can normalize self-promotion, the more we can dismantle this silly myth.

Lack of Role Models

Representation matters every single day. When you don't see anyone you can relate to, you are less willing to do it yourself. So it's important that more women have the courage to promote themselves and to feel more comfortable about it. This is the main reason why I show up on social media, sharing my books and my achievements, and even talking about the topic of self-promotion.

If you want things to change for the better, you have to start with yourself. So I realized that I have to be the one who walks the talk because if I don't, I am a hypocrite. Actions speak louder than words. To be honest, I am still very uncomfortable with self-promotion. If I had a choice, I would be hiding from the world, binge-watching K-dramas and eating ramen noodles. But I also understand that this issue is bigger than me.

So if you know me or have seen me on social media, you may think I have all the confidence in the world. What you don't see is me freaking out before I hit that "post" button. But I make it a habit to keep showing up so that it's less uncomfortable.

It gives me so much joy when women tell me how much it has helped them learn to promote themselves just by seeing my actions. This is why we need more women role models practicing self-promotion. It's how we can create the change we want to see in the world and have more women leaders in every industry.

Self-Sabotage

This is something that I do and I'm not always aware of doing it. When someone gives me a compliment, I turn it down, say mean things to myself, or create the worst-case scenario in my head. Sometimes I don't even realize that the person who is trying to sabotage me the most is me.

Self-sabotage is a behavior that creates problems in daily life and interferes with long-standing goals. Symptoms of self-sabotage include procrastination, self-injury, putting yourself down, comfort eating, and more.[2]

This is another reason why women also stop themselves from self-promotion. The things we tell ourselves stop us from stepping up or showing up to tell the world what we are capable of. The self-sabotaging behavior that is most common for me is procrastination. You might be shocked to hear that, but I am one of those people who will put things off until I have two hours left before the due date, and then I feel like it's too late to go after the things I wish to achieve.

Another one of my self-sabotaging behaviors is comfort eating. Whenever I get rejected a number of times in a row, or I'm frustrated, or I feel demotivated with life, I turn to food for comfort.

Even though I know that what I'm doing is wrong and that eating to run away from my problems isn't helping me, I can't fully stop myself from indulging in comfort eating. I have been able to work through this over the years, but it does still creep up from time to time.

I used to hide this stuff from the world because, as someone who talks publicly about confidence and leadership, these are not the sexy things that I'd want my audience to know. People might think less of me, or I'd feel ashamed for going down this rabbit hole. But I realize that as human beings, we all go through highs and lows no matter what happens in life. So I hope my being able to share the darker side of myself can help you realize that you are not alone and that you too can come out of it.

For years I delayed my own success by sabotaging every opportunity that came my way. Even in my 30s, I thought it was too late for me to become a public speaker because I considered myself too old. I constantly thought someone else who was better than me would get the job done. I filled my head with so many things I thought were wrong about me that I resisted even making the first move.

An article from BetterUp offers a helpful five-step process to stop your self-sabotage:[3]

1. *Develop self-awareness.* Figure out what's stopping you and where it came from. Maybe something happened in your childhood that is creating this self-sabotage. If you ask the right questions, the right answers will appear.
2. *Write it out.* Moments of self-awareness can be fleeting, so it's useful to record insights in a notebook or a notes app on your phone so you won't forget. Journaling is also a great exercise to mind-dump all your thoughts.
3. *Create a plan and do it.* Now that you're aware of what is creating the self-sabotage, create a plan to heal from it and take action—and make it a habit.
4. *Practice mindfulness.* Unpacking this stuff is not always easy or pretty, so it's important to find time to practice

mindfulness through meditation or even just find some quiet time to yourself. Do what works for you. Or consider hiring a coach to help you with this.

5. *Communicate*. You don't have to do this alone. Sharing what you're going through with someone you trust can be a good thing. By sharing my dark moments with you, I feel much better about unpacking the things I go through when it comes to self-sabotage.

Facing Backlash

I know it's not easy to put yourself out there because you can end up being "cancelled" or receiving backlash from haters. Unfortunately, when you put yourself out there, haters are part of the package. Not everyone is going to like what you do or agree with it, but if you have good intentions to make the world a better place for you and your loved ones, then just do it.

Most of the people who hate on you are dealing with their own insecurities and are projecting them on you. And yes, I know it is easier said than done to ignore the haters, because as I try, it still does get to me. So I take the time to feel my feelings, ask myself what lessons I will learn from this, then I go back to my purpose and move on.

When I first dealt with backlash, it really got to me. I would focus on the one bad comment versus the 50 good ones. I became so fixated on the bad comment that I forgot about all the good I have done for others. I had to realize one bad comment is someone's opinion and not my truth. I had to practice letting the haters hate and continue on my mission.

Everyone deals with backlash differently. It's important to have a support system because it makes a big difference when there are people who will be there for you through the ups and downs. Don't ever feel bad that you are feeling a certain way. Learn to acknowledge your feelings, let them go, and move forward. Don't ever hold it in because that makes things worse for you!

How Self-Promotion Is Perceived

When creating a presentation for an organization to talk about how to promote yourself with confidence, I decided to Google the definition of self-promotion. I was pretty surprised that in 2024, this is how Google's dictionary defined it:

> The action of promoting or publicizing oneself or one's activities, especially in a forceful way.

"In a forceful way"? This is a terrible definition! Is sharing your achievements on social media "forceful"? Is including a positive testimonial from a client on your website "forceful"?

I was stunned to think that this is how self-promotion is perceived. Why does self-promotion have to be seen in a negative light when it can be used for good? This is why it's so important to show others that self-promotion can be a positive thing. There's no reason it has to be a forceful way to promote yourself.

Of course, not everyone uses self-promotion for good. So you want to be intentional about how you promote yourself. When you have good intentions, it will never feel forceful, and the right people will be able to sense that you are doing it for the right reasons.

Cultural Norms

Your culture can play a big part in the challenge of promoting yourself. Certain traditions may stop you from showing up. As an Asian woman, I can totally relate, because my culture tells me that self-promotion is shameful and that I should be modest and never boast about my achievements.

But it's not just my culture that imposes these barriers. Most cultures tell women that we shouldn't make noise and should stay in the background. Almost all women face cultural norms that stop them from truly showing up. Perhaps it's the clothes you're told to wear or the words you're allowed to say. No wonder we're too afraid to come out of our shell!

Such cultural norms hurt all women. Most of the time we blindly follow tradition without even knowing why, so it's important to question why we follow them.

An article from consultancy and global network INvolve addresses the difference between individualistic cultures and collective cultures and explores how cultural differences can play a role in self-promotion.[4] When we think of individualistic cultures, we tend to think of North America, where self-promotion is generally considered okay. But if you belong to a collective culture, you tend to do things for the good of the group.

I can relate to this distinction. Since moving to Canada, I learned that I can express my opinions openly without any judgment. When I went back to the Philippines for a vacation with my family, I decided to share my opinions with my great-uncles, who had a different response from what I normally get in Canada. My uncles told me that I was out of line for speaking my mind. What was seen as a norm in Canada was considered a sign of disrespect in another country.

The American Psychological Association defines "cultural norm" this way:[5]

A societal rule, value, or standard that delineates an accepted and appropriate behavior within a culture.

Most of the time, women are limited by the norms their culture tells them to follow. Yet these are not absolute truths but simply certain people's opinions. It's really important to realize how these types of cultural norms can affect women's confidence, which in turn affects self-promotion.

An article in HuffPost explains nine extreme cultural customs that oppress women around the world:[6]

1. *Force-feeding young girls.* For several centuries, obesity has been celebrated in countries with high levels of

malnourishment like Mauritania, a country in northwest Africa, where they practice leblouh, or gavage, force-feeding young girls with high-calorie, unhealthy foods to make them look more desirable for prospective suitors. Girls as young as six are sent to a special camp where they are forced to consume up to 16,000 calories a day. If they do not comply, they are punished by being forced to ingest their own vomit. This practice has led young girls to take drugs, steroids, and animal growth hormones to fatten themselves up. This horrid practice is physical and mental torture.

2. *Devadasis.* In India, this practice means that a person is considered a servant of a deity and the temple. Little girls from very poor families are sent as the servants and most of the time they are sexually assaulted by the people who run the temple or they are forced into prostitution. When the girl reaches puberty, her virginity is auctioned off to the highest bidder. It's really heartbreaking to know that these innocent girls are forced to do something disgusting to appease a man's desire.

3. *Menstruating women removed to cattle sheds.* In some parts of Nepal, women who are menstruating are sent to the cattle sheds, where they sleep with the cows and buffalos, in a practice called Chhaupadi. Women who are menstruating are considered impure and are prohibited from entering their own home or from touching anything and anyone. Many of these cattle sheds have very unhygienic living conditions, such as cow manure and insects. Even though this harmful practice has been outlawed, it is still practiced.

4. *Breast ironing.* In Cameroon and other African countries, mothers pound the breasts of young girls with hot iron tools and/or stones to stop them from growing, because women with large breasts are considered shameful since it is feared they will attract unwanted attention. This very painful custom may start on girls as young as 10 in order to delay their

first sexual encounter and pregnancy. This is child abuse and it risks harmful aftereffects, such as deformation and difficulties with breastfeeding as the girls grow older.

5. *Finger amputation to mourn death.* In Papau, Indonesia, the women of the Dani Tribe are forced to have the top of one of their fingers cut off as a way to mourn the death of family members. This is considered a way to grieve the emotional pain of the permanent loss through death by manifesting it into physical pain. A half hour before the fingertip is cut off, a string is tied around it to make it go numb, then the tip is cauterized after cutting. Even in reading about this procedure, you can feel their pain.

6. *Lip plating.* In Ethiopia, Mursi and Surma women wear large circular wooden and/or clay discs on their lips as a sign of beauty and status. These large discs are inserted in the upper and lower lips of young girls, usually beginning during puberty. Some of the painful procedures include cutting a hole in the lips, removing teeth, and replacing the smaller disc with a larger disc as the lips are stretched out so the woman will receive a larger dowry on her wedding day. This procedure didn't even start as a beauty enhancement but more of a way to keep slave traders away from them.

7. *Sexual cleansing of widows.* In parts of Tanzania, widows go through a ritual of "sexual cleansing" after being inherited by their in-laws after their husband's death. The widow is required to have sexual intercourse with her brother-in-law as a way to remove the soul of her dead spouse. If she does not comply with the sexual cleansing, she is chased out of her own home and is not entitled to receive her husband's property and/or livestock and, even worse, is shunned by the community. Sometimes, a professional cleanser is hired if the male relative refuses to have intercourse with the widow. Think about that: the male relatives get a choice with no consequences, while the women are ridiculed and cast out for refusing to practice this tradition.

8. *Neck rings*. In the rural villages of Myanmar and Thailand, a long slender neck is considered a sign of beauty and grace. Women go through the painful process of wearing up to 20 or 25 rings around their necks to gradually elongate it, starting with girls as young as five. They are allowed to remove the rings only once in their lifetime, during their wedding night. This excruciating procedure has been around for centuries. When my best friend and I visited one of the villages in Thailand where they practice this, it was painful just to observe it.

9. *Genital mutilation*. In parts of Africa, the Middle East, and Asia, genital mutilation is still prevalent. In the belief that it will reduce libido and prevent sexual debauchery, young girls are subjected to partial or complete mutilation of their external genitalia. The materials used in this heinous act are often not sterilized and no anesthesia is used. While genital mutilation is banned in most places, it continues in some cultures and sometimes a trained health worker will end up conducting the procedure.

These dangerous cultural customs affect everything a girl or woman does, from the way she thinks about herself to being shamed for simply being female because of cultural beliefs. These examples are extreme, but they highlight the ways that women continue to be oppressed around the world. If you are continually told you are not good enough or are second-class to men, then you cannot show up for yourself or for others.

Women Bear More Responsibilities Than Men

Most women are not able to simply concentrate on their job or business. They are the ones who have to pick up the kids, make dinner, ensure the kids get their homework done, give them a bath, read the bedtime story, and put them to bed.

And that is only during the second half of the day. Mornings are consumed with getting the kids up, making breakfast, packing lunches, dropping them off at school—all before going into the office to prepare for a big presentation. When you have to do all of the household maintenance plus your career, it takes a toll. You end up drained and exhausted and it's not bedtime yet.

As we've discussed before, most men have the luxury to concentrate on their jobs and businesses. In Chapter 1, I mentioned how a certain guru tells people that in order to succeed, they must hustle 12–14 hours a day. Men generally have the luxury to do that because their partners run the household and take care of the kids.

What if you're a single mother? Trying to do it all is absolutely exhausting! I applaud the single moms out there; I know you're doing your best, and you need to know that you are killing it!

Because women bear more responsibilities than men, the gender burnout gap means women have suffered higher levels of burnout than men for years, and that gap has doubled since 2019.[7] Some of the reasons this gap exists is that women are less likely to be promoted, more likely to head single-parent families, and more likely to take low-paying or unpaid jobs. When you are responsible for everything and everyone else, when do you have the time to advocate for yourself?

Let's talk about some strategies to help women be more empowered to promote themselves.

Strategies for Effective Self-Promotion for Women

Here are some effective strategies that women can use to promote themselves while building their confidence in the process.

Have a Big Purpose

It's important to have a purpose that everyone can relate to and be a part of. When you know that self-promotion is not really just about yourself—it's really about your purpose—you are more willing to put yourself out there, even if it's scary.

If I had a choice, I would not be putting myself out there. I'd rather be doing things in the background and not be seen. Self-promotion is still very uncomfortable for me. I continue to question whether to press the "post" button. But I also realize that I have to lead by example because there is a woman out there who needs to see that it's okay to promote her products and services. Growing up in an Asian culture didn't help either, since Asian women are told to stay in the background and not make noise.

By showing up and promoting myself, I saw the change in others just by observing women promoting themselves for the first time on social media. And that helps me keep on going even when it's uncomfortable. So figure out a purpose as to why you want to start promoting yourself, and that purpose doesn't have to be the same as mine. Maybe you want to start because you have a daughter and you want to show her that anything is possible when you put yourself out there. That is something many mothers can relate to.

Even though this is all about self-promotion, it's a lot easier when it's not just about you. Your actions are what will empower others to do the same thing. Figure out what your purpose is and don't worry if you don't know it right away. As you take action, you are also evolving, so your purpose may change. When I first started on my path, I had no idea what my purpose was, but taking imperfect action helped me figure out my purpose.

Self-Promotion as Leadership Building

Most people don't realize this, but self-promotion helps you become a better leader. It took me a while to understand the many leadership qualities I developed once I started promoting myself.

When you are your biggest advocate and cheerleader and you are out there telling the world what you are capable of, this also tells others some important things:

- You are a qualified person for the position at work or for that promotion.
- You are confident in your abilities.
- You know that you have a product and/or service that will change someone's life for the better.
- You are breaking barriers.
- You are an innovator.
- You know your worth and value.
- You are trailblazing and opening doors for others by going first.
- You become better at communication the more you do it.
- You learn to become more courageous and confident.
- You show deep passion for your work.
- You become a better speaker.

And all these are qualities of a leader. When you can see how self-promotion is part of building your leadership presence, you are more inclined to take action.

Utilize Testimonials and Endorsements

When you go out there and promote yourself, it doesn't always have to come from you. You can utilize the words of others with your audience or even with your boss if you are going after that promotion.

If you are an entrepreneur, client testimonials can showcase how good your products and/or services are. Ask clients for a testimonial. The worst that can happen is that they ghost you, which they're unlikely to do if you really made their life better.

As an author, one of the things I did with my first book was ask for book reviews on Amazon. Of course, I asked the people who found value in the book to provide a great review. Just remember that sometimes life gets in the way and you have to give a little nudge or reminder to submit the book review.

It was easy to share this very positive Amazon review with my audience because it came from someone who enjoyed reading the book:

A powerful and empowering book that resonates deeply with anyone striving for self-empowerment and authenticity. I found Sheena's insights particularly poignant. Through a blend of personal anecdotes, interviews, and practical advice, Sheena illuminates the path towards self-confidence with wisdom drawn from her own journey and the experiences of remarkable women she's encountered.

What makes this book truly exceptional is its intersectional perspective, acknowledging the unique challenges faced by Asian women in cultivating self-confidence within both cultural and societal contexts. She offers guidance that is both culturally sensitive and universally applicable.

The Tao of Self Confidence is more than just a book; it's a manifesto for embracing one's true self and reclaiming personal power. It serves as a beacon of inspiration for women of marginalized communities and individuals of all backgrounds seeking to overcome self-doubt and embrace their inherent worth. Sheena's work is a testament to the transformative power of self-love, resilience, and embracing one's authentic voice in the journey towards empowerment and inclusion.

If you work in corporate, start asking your peers about the good qualities you possess and create a document with those responses. If your peers allow you to share what they said about you with your boss or you utilize that when you apply for a promotion, that will help you look like a great candidate to move up to the next role.

Even better, make sure you have a LinkedIn profile and look for the section called Recommendations, where your connections can leave a good review about you. LinkedIn is the number one professional social media platform, so if you don't have a LinkedIn profile, create one as soon as possible, or if you have one but don't really use it, be sure to refresh it. To pay it forward, remember to leave a review on LinkedIn for the people who gave you positive recommendations.

Cultivate an Online Presence

The internet has allowed people to expand their horizons to literally reach the whole world, which is why it's important to create an online presence. You want to be sure you have something to show when people look you up.

Many people don't realize how important it is to utilize your online real estate to promote yourself and be seen as a leader and expert in your field. So be sure to take full advantage of your social media accounts, set up a website, get on podcast interviews, and more.

When traveling from Toronto to Atlanta to attend a conference, I was stuck at the customs office, and the customs officer asked me why I was entering the United States. After about 15–20 minutes of interrogation, he Googled my name. I was a little nervous when he stayed silent for a while because I didn't know what the outcome was going to be.

When he was done with the Google search, I was pleasantly shocked when he announced, "Wow, I didn't know that I was talking to *the* Sheena Yap Chan!" I get a little embarrassed when people say things like that, and I'm still trying to get used to. He said that my resume was impressive and that I was good to go.

If I hadn't built my online presence, it would have been a different story. The customs officer would have continued asking me questions, or perhaps even stopped me from entering the United States if there was nothing online to back up what I had told him.

Utilize Storytelling in Your Self-Promotion

One of the greatest things you can do is incorporate storytelling when you promote yourself. Stories are a powerful way to connect with your audience. I always incorporate storytelling in my content because people want to make that connection.

If you're concerned that your story will not be effective, keep in mind that it will likely connect with at least one person who may be in a similar situation as you. You are doing a disservice to the world if you keep your story to yourself.

I know it can be scary to share your story because I was in that spot too when I first started my journey. I was terrified of sharing my story because I was afraid people might laugh at me, but the results turned out to be the total opposite. People sent me private messages and emails to say how my story resonated with them. And from that moment on, I realized that I had to share my story so that others can see what is possible for themselves.

Companies frequently use storytelling in their marketing campaigns and commercials because they understand how powerful it can be to connect with their audience and in turn convert into sales. One of my favorite campaigns that is very skilled at using storytelling is Jollibee, the biggest fast food chain in the Philippines. Not even McDonalds can defeat Jollibee.

Jollibee is known for their burgers, fried chicken, and other Filipino dishes and treats. Throughout the Philippines there seems to be a Jollibee restaurant at every corner, always packed with people. They have now expanded to the United States, Canada, Europe, and beyond.

Every Valentine's Day, Jollibee releases a series of three videos on YouTube called Kwentong Jollibee that tell a story about love and how Jollibee is part of their love story. (*Kwentong* means "story" in Tagalog.) Some of these videos are real tearjerkers. I remember one video where a son organizes a Valentine's date for his mom at Jollibee. You can hear the father instructing the son how to decorate the restaurant for the date. When the mother enters, she is escorted to the table that was set up by her son. He gives the mother a tablet to watch a video of the father, and we learn he has passed away from cancer. The father wishes his wife a Happy Valentine's

Day, apologizes for not being able to show up for the date, and says that their son will be her Valentine's date from now on. The son gives her a bouquet of flowers and they have dinner together. Who knew that a two-and-a-half-minute video would make me cry so much?

The video series received a ton of views and went viral, which in turn boosted Jollibee's sales. It's the number one fast food chain the Philippines for a reason. So check out how companies utilize storytelling for their campaigns and model off of them. This can help you feel better about self-promotion and realize that it's not tacky. Everyone loves to hear a good story!

Share Your Achievements

Growing up, I was always told never to share my achievements because it was seen as bragging. So for the longest time, I never shared anything. But over the years I realized that by not sharing my achievements, I was doing a disservice to others who are seeking representation and/or a mentor.

So I started sharing my achievements to my audience on social media. As someone who talks about having more representation, it had to start with me, even if it still felt uncomfortable most of the time. The more I shared my achievements, the more people would send me private messages saying how this inspired them to start their own businesses, begin their public speaking career, or even go for that promotion.

Even people with more influence and income than me would send messages commending me for putting myself out there because it's rarely seen, especially in Asian culture. They appreciated the fact that I was out there and sharing my achievements because they were too shy to do it. I have spoken to eight-figure female earners who were not comfortable telling people that they were the CEO of their companies!

There are so many reasons why it's important to share your achievements, but the most important is to show women what is possible for themselves. Women are often too shy to share what they have accomplished for fear of being laughed at, but every time I have shared my achievements, 98% of the time I have been celebrated. And when I see others sharing their achievements, I celebrate them as well. It's very rare that people will hate on me because of what I've shared, and when that does happen, I hit the "Block" button. When you share your achievements, it's also proof that you produced a desired result, which in turn can build your confidence, not to mention bring more business your way.

The first time I shared any achievement was through my podcast. Now I share every single milestone I ever hit, whether it is a testimonial or hitting a significant download number. Because I constantly share the milestones, so many more people started listening to the podcast, and right now my podcast is in the top 0.5% most popular podcasts in the world, which is mind boggling to me.[8] I have had this podcast for almost 10 years and to know these results is such an amazing surprise and indeed an achievement that needs to be shared out to the world.

So I hope that, starting today, you will begin sharing your achievements to your audience, no matter how big or small they may be. There is someone out there who is cheering you on and is inspired by your actions.

Product Placement

Are you a K-drama fan like me? If you are, then you've noticed that every K-drama features some sort of product placement. Some of these placements are shameless in promoting the product on the show, which makes me laugh because I think it's brilliant.

K-dramas have become a global phenomenon, especially during and since the pandemic. So many people around the world are watching K-dramas that companies will pay big money to have their products placed on these highly rated shows. A *New York Times* article mentioned that companies spent $114 million on South Korea TV Network for product placements in 2018, a 15% increase from the previous year.[9]

And it's not only K-dramas that make big money from product placements. Hollywood does the same thing. Another *New York Times* article stated that product placement was a $23 billion industry in 2022, which was up by 14% since 2020.[10]

I utilize product placements in my own business, whether it's sharing my logo, wearing something red, or pimping out my book. I literally bring my book everywhere with me because I never know when the right opportunity may occur to take a photo that I can use in my marketing.

Even when I'm at the coffee shop doing my work or writing this book, I have a copy of my first book placed on the table because so many people walk by me or are in line to order their coffee. They happen to see my book on the table and start asking questions about it. Isn't it better if they ask you about your product and you can talk to them about it?

Start utilizing product placement in your self-promotion. Self-promotion doesn't always mean you have to show your face. It can be the products you sell or the logo you have created for yourself to share with your audience. Before social media, the rule of marketing was that a person would need to see your product at least seven times before they made a buying decision. In today's world of social media, people need to see it at 25–30 times before they make a buying decision. This is why product placement is a great way to get it out there.

Seek Help

There's no reason why you have to learn to promote yourself on your own. If you want to promote yourself effectively, seek help from someone who has been there and done that. Check out people of influence who have learned to master the art of self-promotion, or hire a coach to help you. There are so many free and paid resources to help you through this process. You can also check out the Tao Queens (https://taoqueens.com) and Queens Makers (https://queenmaker.ai) programs, which may provide some help in this area.

As women, we feel like we have to do every single thing on our own because we have been programmed to be the superwoman in everything. That's a myth, and when you can move past that and seek and accept help, it makes your life so much easier.

When I did a presentation on how to promote yourself with confidence for the New York Public Library, the audience loved it. In fact, one attendee shared her upcoming webinar in the Zoom chat because I encouraged them to apply what they had learned during the presentation. It was great to see so many people loving the content and learning new ways of self-promotion.

I hope this chapter has helped you see self-promotion as empowering. It really is a great way to build your confidence and be seen as a leader in your industry when you see the benefits of self-promotion and just how far you can go with it.

Pick one strategy that I mentioned in the chapter and start utilizing it in your own business and/or career. Learning all of this is great, but it's even better when you apply it in your own journey. Make a commitment of 30 days to promote yourself every day and see what your results are after the month. Write down the whole experience so you can see your progress from day 1 to day 30.

Now let's get to the next chapter, which is all about the confidence era, because it's your time to shine!

6

The Confidence Era

An article in the *New York Post* stated that almost half of women believe that they are just entering into their confidence era, and that the average age of 38 is when women start stepping into their confidence and knowing who they truly are as a person. This was determined by a survey of 2,000 women over the age of 35 conducted by OnePoll. The article also mentioned that authenticity will have a 46% further boost by 2028. Currently about 67% of women are always looking for ways to be more confident in certain areas of their lives.[1]

Here are more findings from the study:

- 29% of women feel like their true self during their teenage years.
- 21% of women ages 19–23 struggle embracing who they truly are.
- 64% of women are more sure of themselves now than compared to their younger self.
- Women are hoping to be more confident in four areas: socializing (54%), how they look (49%), their career (45%), and their hobbies or passions (41%).

- The top three ways that women boost their confidence are spending time with loved ones (49%), laughing or making jokes with family and friends (43%), or trying a new hairstyle (31%).
- 61% of women have a positive view of aging.

I loved reading that women are entering into their confidence era. I believe that I truly stepped into my own confidence in my 40s, when I started to love myself for who I really am and decided to go after the things I want, even if it meant not knowing where to begin.

This is also the time when my gray hairs are starting to come out and I am just embracing aging as something positive instead of something negative. While I still go through bad days, self-doubt, imposter syndrome, and more, I am surer than ever of who I truly am and doing my best to show up for others.

It can be really scary to share your true self, especially when women are prone to getting more ridicule and criticism than men, but it's necessary to show up as your authentic and confident self so we can normalize this for all women. The more we can build confidence in women, the more positive impact we can create in this world because I truly believe that women are phenomenal and what is really stopping them is questioning their capabilities. So in this chapter I want to share ways for you to start stepping into your confidence era so you can show up as your best and authentic self. When you become confident and authentic, you also become unstoppable!

In the words of the iconic Diana Ross, it's time to step out and starting singing, "I'm coming out! I want the world to know, gotta let it show."

So let's step into our confidence era!

Train Your Brain for Confidence

Confidence really starts with how you see yourself and what you are thinking. Your mind is very powerful, so anything you see or hear can affect your confidence. You have to think of your brain as your computer hard drive. If you feed it with good things, then it works fine, but if you feed it with a virus, then it won't work as well.

If you constantly tell yourself that you are not good enough to be an entrepreneur or to go for that promotion, then you are not going to do it. This is why it's important to train your brain to have confidence. When you learn to believe in yourself and in your abilities, then you will have the confidence to go out there and crush those goals or live your dream life.

So how do you start training your brain for confidence? Here's some strategies that can help:

Take advantage of neuroplasticity.

- Neuroplasticity is the brain's ability to change or adapt. Your brain is so much more powerful than you realize that when used for good, you can move the brain's function from a damaged area to an undamaged area. Your memories and experiences that your brain has stored can also change the way you see and do things, such as learning a new skill. There are so many benefits to neuroplasticity, such as helping you learn new things, enhancing existing cognitive capabilities, recovering from strokes and traumatic brain injuries, strengthening the areas where function is lost or has declined, and boosting your brain fitness. While it can have negative effects on the brain, leading to such things as substance abuse or trauma, it is important to practice it for good, such as learning something new, getting plenty of rest, exercising on a regular basis, and also practicing mindfulness. Playing brain games can also help improve your brain's neuroplasticity.[2]

Practice mental fitness.

- While it's important to work out and exercise your body to be healthy, it's also important to exercise your brain so that you can improve your memory, cognitive abilities, mood, and more. Brain fitness must be incorporated in your daily work to boost your confidence, but how do you practice it? The most important thing is to be aware of your thoughts and how they affect you. When you can learn to identify what thoughts are stopping you from being confident, then you can start to find ways to solve them. Personal development is something that must be done in your mental fitness journey because this is where you develop positive new thought patterns that will help you boost your confidence. You can read a book, listen to a podcast, or check out interviews on YouTube of successful people. When you can practice this on a daily basis, your confidence will soar.

Practice positive self-talk.

- What you say to yourself matters. You may not even realize that the things you say to yourself can actually hurt your confidence. If you are constantly telling yourself that you are no good, you are also programming your brain to think the same. This is why positive self-talk is so important, because you are training your brain with positive thought patterns that will help you become more confident in yourself and in your abilities. Start by saying positive affirmations, listening to positive audio, or even using positive self-talk audio where you listen to positive statements you say about yourself. You can record your own audio or you can listen to people whose voice you think is of a higher influence that you would pay attention to.

I hope these strategies can help you start to train your brain to be more confident. When you apply this in your daily routine, you will see how far your brain can stretch and see what you can accomplish.

Visualize Having Confidence

If you want to step into your confidence era, it's important to start visualizing what that looks like for you. Most of the time, we tend to worry about the future, not knowing that we can use that energy to focus on how amazing our future can be through the practice of visualization.

I used to be the person who always worried about the future or thought about the worst-case scenario. I would often ask myself, "What if I go out there and everything goes wrong?" But what if I ask myself the opposite question: "What if I go out there and everything goes right?" Isn't it wild how much we are conditioned to always think about the negative impact instead of the positive impact of an event that hasn't even happened yet? This is why practicing visualization is so important: because you can change the way you see your future in an instant.

Start seeing in your mind what your life would be like if you had the confidence to go after your dream life, go for that promotion, or open your first business. This is such a powerful exercise that is often underutilized. You have to believe it before you see it; you have to train your brain that you already have the confidence to be the woman that you are meant to be.

So how do you practice visualization? This article from Calm will help you with several approaches:[3]

- *Safe place visualization exercise.* Your mind is so powerful, and it's important to create a safe place in your head where you can practice visualization. I remember doing this exercise at a personal development seminar in Hawaii. The instructor had us create a place where we felt the safest and could get our mindset right. You can look through photos in magazines to get ideas for the type of safe space you want to visualize for the amazing things that will come your way. Maybe your safe place is the beach or a penthouse on the 50th floor of a high-rise building. Pick something that works for you and where you feel calm and safe.
- *Color breathing.* This practice teaches you to use colors as you breathe in and out. Each color you inhale and exhale represents an emotion that you are going through. Maybe the color

blue means you are calm and the color pink means you are happy. Choose a color that will represent confidence when you are practicing this visualization technique.

- *Loving-kindness meditation.* This practice involves visualizing that you are sending happy thoughts and wishes to someone. It can be your family, friends, a stranger, or yourself. It's important to send yourself positive thoughts and wishes, especially if you have been your own worst enemy for so long. You have to show yourself more love and kindness. You would never treat your family or best friend badly, so why would you do that to yourself?

- *Visualization with affirmations.* I love affirmations because they help me get back on track when I start to doubt myself or I don't value my worth. When I first started saying affirmations to myself, I admit it felt awkward because it was something that I'd never done before. But with practice, I felt more comfortable because it calms me down when my anxiety starts to act up. And I don't say a hundred affirmations, I literally say only three affirmations to myself: "I am loved," "I am worthy," and "I am enough." I keep saying this over and over again to myself until I feel like myself again. Feel free to use these affirmations or you can come up with three affirmations that resonate with you.

- *Body scan mediation.* Our body is our vessel, and it's important to take good care of it. By doing a body meditation scan, you are able to focus the energy flow of your body, which promotes balance and vitality. It's a great exercise before bedtime and also helps reduce stress. To practice body scan mediation, envision healing energy entering from the top of your head and slowly moving down to your toes. Imagine this energy traveling from the top to the bottom of your body, soothing any discomfort so you can feel more relaxed.

- *Creative visualization.* This type of visualization is very powerful since it can give you the boost of confidence you are looking for. Creative visualization involves visualizing your goals and desires already being achieved. You might picture yourself creating your first six-figure business or getting that promotion at work. You can even write it down: describe in as much detail as possible how the goal was achieved and what you are feeling the moment you achieved that goal. This is a great way for you to see that you can achieve your goals and what you visualize can become a reality.

Visualization is truly powerful and many successful people utilize this practice because they know that once they can see it in their minds, they will find a way to make it happen. Try one of these visualization practices that aligns with you today.

Practice Low-Risk Self-Confidence

I saw an article in *Forbes* that talks about practicing low-risk self-confidence and I love this idea, especially when it comes to building confidence.[4] Most people think that you have to make big leaps to become confident when that's far from the truth.

When you practice low-risk self-confidence, you choose something that is easy to do that will help you build your confidence little by little. Let's say you have a job interview and you ask someone you know to help you prepare, like your sister or your best friend. This is a great way to practice your self-confidence because you are taking it one step at a time. Even if you get it wrong during your preparation, your friends and family will be able to give you feedback on how to improve your skills so that you can be ready for the interview.

You can also explore what a calculated risk would feel like. A great example of this would be when you launch a product and/or service, you might pick 10 people to work with at a beta price (low introductory price for being the first users) as a way to test the product and get feedback from the clients who worked with you. This helps you figure out what went wrong and how you can improve on the product and/or service for the price that you want to charge.

I didn't even realize that I did this in my own journey. I was presenting a webinar about building confidence and someone from the audience asked me how I was able to get over 800 women to be interviewed on my podcast. When I first started my podcast, I had no influence at all. Nobody knew who I was and I had to figure out how I was going to get women to be interviewed. So I started by asking my friends and I am so grateful that they said yes. Little by little I started doing outreach to others I thought would be great candidates for the podcast and slowly I began reaching out to people with bigger influence and incomes for interviews. This was how I practiced low-risk self-confidence, by reaching out to my friends first to be guests and then I started building up my confidence from there.

I always say that it's the small actionable daily steps that yield the big results. So find some ways for you to start practicing low-risk self-confidence in your life. Maybe you want to start a business and you practice your pitch to your best friend or your partner, or you want to run a marathon so you start with running one kilometer. The most important part is to start practicing today.

Accept Your True Self

As a woman in her 40s, I feel like there's so many changes happening with me. My bones ache more and of course my gray hairs are starting to appear now more than ever. In the first chapter, I mentioned how ageism is something that women in their 40s and older have to deal with, thinking that we have hit a certain expiration date.

There is no such thing as an expiration date on what we can contribute, and like I mentioned before, everything that I ever wanted to achieve in my life actually happened in my 40s. I feel like this is just the beginning and I always want to promote that women can thrive in their 40s, 50s, 60s, and beyond. If you are a woman over 40 and you want to sport that bikini, then you go ahead and do it. Life is too short to wear the opinions of others.

And I live my life sharing what it means to be a woman in her 40s. It means my gray hairs growing out, and I'm loving every strand.

My body might not be as fit as it was in my 20s but I love my body anyway. I show up more myself, meaning the good, the bad, and the ugly, and I'm able to unconditionally love myself because of it. Being in my 40s also means that I am thriving because I am able to have more confidence and I can define my own happiness and success. The gray hairs and wrinkles symbolize the struggles I had to overcome to get to where I am today. So I celebrate it instead of thinking my life is over because I hit a certain age.

This also means that I show up as my imperfect self. I share the highs and lows of my life because I know so many people are going through their own highs and lows in their journey as well. This is really what it means to step into your confidence era; it's about stepping into your true self, including your flaws. Social media has given us so many masks to hide our true self, but it doesn't really help us if we hide. The more we can show up as our true self, the more others will follow. We can create a wave of more women accepting themselves for who they truly are, and that is the most beautiful thing a woman can wear.

Prioritize *You*

Women are seen as natural-born caretakers with a maternal instinct (whether or not you have kids). Women are conditioned to be selfless and to take care of everyone else, to the point that we forget to take care the most important person in our life: ourselves!

There is nothing wrong with taking care of others, but you also have to learn to prioritize yourself. This means taking time for yourself and being able to take care of yourself, and not feeling that you're being selfish for doing that. If you don't take the time to prioritize *you*, you may be limiting yourself, which can also limit your confidence.

I know it's easier said than done, especially since it is what you have been taught all of your life to do. This is why it takes work on your part to unlearn this belief that you have to sacrifice yourself for others and start learning new beliefs about you. Start learning to enjoy your own company, take time for yourself to reflect, and learn to say no to people and things that don't serve you.

Prioritizing yourself also means respecting yourself. You do this by understanding your worth and your value. If you don't respect yourself, then you will attract people who will walk all over you or take advantage of you. I don't want this for you, I want you to realize your worth and what you bring to the table.

When you learn to prioritize yourself, you also start to attract the right people into your life, because you learn what you will or will not tolerate for yourself. Your life becomes better in the process because you have less stress and anxiety about what other people think of you, and you are happier because you are doing things that give you joy.

Create a routine where you can prioritize yourself. Start by setting aside 5–10 minutes of "me time" as a bare minimum. I know you have a busy life but it's important to set that time to rest and recharge. As you come to recognize the value of that time, however brief, you'll soon add another 5, 10, or 15 minutes to really focus on yourself.

Start Messy

If there is at least one thing you take away from this book, I would like it to be this. It's okay to start messy in your journey. It will never be perfect. We often hold back while we wait for the perfect moment to start, but five years later we'll still be waiting because that perfect moment hasn't come along yet.

That was me. I started my podcast in 2015 and for five years I had no clue about how to monetize it. I kept waiting for the perfect strategy and the perfect moment to start monetizing. I continued to procrastinate and resist starting because that perfect moment hadn't come along yet, so after five years I was still stuck at the same place. I'm sharing this painful truth because I think it's very important for you to realize you're not alone in this struggle and it's all part of the process.

Here's the truth: your journey is going to be a hot mess and that is totally okay. There will be moments where you will be happy and there will be moments where you will want to cry out of frustration. It's through the messy parts where we can learn more about ourselves and build confidence along the way.

Starting messy is where you will learn from your mistakes, make decisions on the fly, and make change when it's necessary. Mistakes are inevitable and that is just part of your journey. Sometimes your mistakes can lead you to your biggest opportunity. In the real world, mistakes can be a good thing, and I have made *plenty* of mistakes along the way.

I remember when my mentor started asking me all the things I did to get to where I am today. Part of me felt so uncomfortable telling him what I did because I know I made so many mistakes in my journey. But instead of telling me what I did wrong, he told me how I only knew what I only knew and he was still impressed that I was able to accomplish so many things regardless of the mistakes I made. I was grateful for this feedback, which helped me realize that all the mistakes I made in my journey also led to me to creating solutions for others who are going through a similar situation.

You don't have to know everything in order to start. Many people become known as "accidental" entrepreneurs because they turned their business into a success. Some of these people had no experience or education in their field but managed to make a successful career out of it.

Here are some stories of women entrepreneurs who started without knowledge and/or experience and still became a success:[5]

- *Arlan Hamilton, founder and managing partner, Backstage Capital.* Arlan Hamilton didn't even know what a VC was in 2010 because she used to work in the music industry. She decided to start her VC firm because she was fascinated with the industry, so she began by learning how to set one up. Through her research, she learned that 90% of VC and angel funding was awarded to white men. This caught Arlan off guard since she is a gay Black woman and had no connections with anyone in the VC world. But that didn't stop her. During the time she started building her own firm, she was homeless; she attended pitch meetings during the day and slept on the floor of the San Francisco International Airport during the night. Arlan received her first investor check in 2015, for $25,000, which gave her the means to launch Backstage Capital to support women, BIPOC, and LGBTQ+ entrepreneurs. To date, Backstage Capital has invested about $20 million dollars in about 200 companies. Apart from Backstage Capital, Arlan also started Backstage Studio, which offers mentorship to train the next generation of underestimated entrepreneurs.

- *Turia Pitt, burn survivor, athlete, author, mindset coach.* Turia Pitt's story is truly inspiring. In 2011, she was running a 100 km marathon when she was caught in a grassfire. Doctors thought she would not survive. Not only did she have severe burns over 65% of her body, but she also lost seven fingers and went through over 200 surgeries in a span of two years. Despite her situation, Turia ended up becoming a three-time bestselling author and has created an online course called School of Champions that has helped over 40,000 people around the world realize their true potential. Less than five years after her accident, she completed the Ironman challenge in Hawaii, which is considered the world's most challenging triathlon.
- *Jane Lu, co-founder of Showpo.* Jane Lu and a friend started Showpo (a woman's fashion, homeware, and accessories company) out of her parents' garage while she was $60,000 in debt. Before that she had worked as a financial analyst at the prestigious Ernst & Young accounting firm. While that might be a dream for many, it wasn't Jane's dream. She was unhappy so she decided to quit and do something totally different. After founding Showpo, Jane started making money within two months through social media and content marketing.

Years later, Jane's business partner wanted to leave the business so Jane bought out her shares and decided to take the company exclusively online. Jane continued to invest in her business, becoming a millionaire at the age of 27. In 2020, Showpo hit $100 million dollars with no external funding.

These women's stories offer proof that you can start messy and still be a success. It takes confidence on your part to know that you have what it takes to make it happen. These women all started messy but still came out on top. Stories like these inspire me to continue the work I do because it's necessary to show you what is possible for yourself.

Trust Your Intuition

Women are generally more intuitive than men. A HuffPost article reported on a study about men and women's brain connectivity. The study showed that men are wired to be more logical in their thinking, while women are better at interpreting social phenomena, including social cues, because they have more neural connections in the brain than men.[6]

And as a woman, you know when something feels right because there are signs all around that show you the way but you hesitate to take action because you are afraid you could be wrong. This fear might even lead you to go out of your way to find something wrong to prevent yourself from starting.

And sometimes when you act on that intuition, what you pictured in your head is the total opposite of what actually happened. So part of you thinks that you took the wrong action, not realizing that you are still on the right path because when you look back at that moment, you will understand why everything happened the way it happened.

At many times in my life I knew that my current situation wasn't going anywhere but part of me still wanted to hold on to it out of fear that there was nothing better, especially in matters of the heart. I'd fall in love with a guy, see many red flags that pop up, and ignore them because I decided he was the one, not realizing there were better choices out there. With my ex, I knew deep in my heart that he wasn't the one for me but I held onto him for so long because I thought there was no other guy out there who would love me. I was so afraid of losing him and did everything in my power to keep him, only to lose him in the end. If I had followed my intuition and just let him go the first time I felt it, my life would have been a lot easier. But the experiences we go through in life are either a lesson, a blessing, or both.

I did the same thing in my entrepreneurial journey. I would join a company I thought was good for me when it was actually the total opposite. Part of me would know something was off and it wasn't aligned with my values, but another part of me didn't want to be seen as a failure, so I stayed with the company for years before I finally quit. All the red flags were there but I decided to ignore them until I couldn't ignore them anymore. Had I just decided to quit the first time my intuition gave me a nudge, I would have been able to save a lot of money in the process. But I am still grateful for these experiences because they taught me a lot about myself and led me to learn to follow my intuition.

Here are some things you can do to start trusting your intuition:

- *Take a chance on trusting your intuition.* You never know until you try. Will you get it right the first time? Maybe not, but by taking a chance, you can figure out where you went wrong and correct it for the next time you trust your intuition. Learning to trust your intuition will be messy, and you have to be okay with the mess because it can lead you to the answers you are looking for.
- *Be in nature.* Sometimes when I get overwhelmed or feel like my mental health is deteriorating, I go out for a morning jog where I can mind-dump every thought I have in my head. Being outside in nature calms me down, and I can trust my intuition more because I was able to clear my head.

- *Trust that sometimes you just know.* When you know something is off, an unexplained feeling will arise because your intuition is trying to tell you something. Maybe your stomach starts to churn, something pops up in front of your face out of nowhere, or your emotions are more heightened than usual. It's important to take note of it or even write down what you're feeling in that moment so you can be aware of it the next time a similar situation happens.

Of course, there are other ways to practice trusting your intuition, but these are three simple ways you can start.

Seize the Opportunities That Come Your Way

Life presents you with so many opportunities that sometimes you are too afraid to seize one because you're afraid of failing, or you still feel unworthy, or maybe you're worried about committing because you think a better opportunity might come along. Sometimes you just have to say yes even if you have no clue how you'll make it happen.

I met a woman online during the pandemic lockdown who is now one of my closest friends. I was referred to her by one of my podcast guests and when we went on Zoom for the first time, she started talking about the *Women Who BossUp* book series and mentioned that we should create a book highlighting Asian women.

When she told me this idea, I agreed, even though I had no clue about publishing a book or even finding the women to be part of it. I saw the vision and I knew that this book had to happen because there are so few books that highlight Asian women's stories.

And so my friend and I were committed to making this book happen even if it took a year to launch it. Thankfully, *Asian Women Who BossUp* launched in February 2021 and hit the Amazon bestseller list. *Asian Women Who BossUp* is the reason I am writing this book for you. It taught me how to show up for myself and for others. It led me to other opportunities I never thought possible, like being an author for Wiley. I am so grateful that I took that Zoom call at the height of the pandemic and said yes to the opportunity. I can't even imagine what my life would be like if I had turned that down.

Of course, not all opportunities are good opportunities, so this is where trusting your intuition comes into play. I couldn't explain why I said yes to the book, I just knew I had to do it even though I didn't know what I was getting into. I knew in my heart that it was going to be a good thing, and I'm glad I trusted myself enough to seize the opportunity. Other opportunities have also come my way that I've accepted without knowing what's going to happen. My next "yes" was creating the Tao Queens and Queen Makers program, which I was nervous and excited about at the same time. You can also consult other people about opportunities or read reviews. I still do that as well as a way to solidify what my intuition is telling me.

Now that you've seen some of the ways you can step into your confidence era, pick at least one strategy to implement in your own journey and try it for 30 days. Document your progress during that time so you can see the changes in your confidence level from the beginning through day 30.

You can also grab some free gifts to accelerate your confidence era at https://taoqueens.com/gift. There is free content to read on the site and even free downloads on confidence-building for your journey.

Building confidence takes work. You will have good days and not-so-good days. You will run into roadblocks and challenges but having confidence-building strategies in at your fingertips will help you bounce back and continue moving forward, especially when it comes to leadership, which we'll discuss in the next chapter.

7

The Benefits of More Women in Leadership

HAVING MORE WOMEN in leadership is indeed a benefit not only for women, but for the whole world. Women are natural-born caregivers, they instinctively tend to know what's best for everyone in general, and they are more intuitive, which means knowing what the world needs.

With the current status of the world, we definitely need more women in leadership roles. In this chapter, you will see the positive benefits when it comes to having more women leaders.

Notable Women Leaders in History

I think it's important to highlight women from the past who have been able to open the doors for us because it's not always easy to be the trailblazer. So here are some notable women leaders who paved the way.

Yuri Kochiyama

Yuri Kochiyama was a Japanese American civil rights activist who dedicated her life to elevating the voices for underrepresented groups. Her life as an activist stemmed from her own experiences when she and her family were sent to a Japanese internment camp in Arkansas during World War II. The FBI deemed Kochiyama's father a national threat, and while he was in custody his health suffered. He passed away shortly after he was released from custody.

Kochiyama was involved in many organizations that help fight for equality and one of the most notable events was when she and Malcolm X fought side by side for civil rights. The solidarity of two cultures seen in the fellowship between Kochiyama and Malcolm X highlights how important it is to work together to move mountains and fight the injustices we still face today.

Kochiyama was part of organizations such as Asian Americans for Action and Young Lords' Party. She also hosted community-driven meetings, penned newsletters, and led planning around other human rights efforts from her apartment in New York City. Women like Kochiyama help us see the importance of being a voice for others, not only for our own community but for all underrepresented communities.[1]

Eleanor Roosevelt

Eleanor Roosevelt was known as the "First Lady of the World" and she used her status to promote women's empowerment. Her many notable achievements helped change the course of history for women. One of them was holding the first all-female press conference when she became the first lady. She encouraged women to share their stories and defied segregation laws by sitting between whites and Blacks at the Southern Conference for Human Welfare in Birmingham, Alabama. Eleanor also spoke for the United Nations.[2]

I was fortunate to take a tour of the White House with some friends when I went to DC to speak at the Department of Transportation. The room that stood out to me the most was the Red Room.

Of course, I loved the room because red is my favorite color, but also because that room became a site for social change. Back then it was taboo for women reporters to attend White House press conferences, but Eleanor Roosevelt changed that by holding press conferences for women reporters in the Red Room.[3]

Madam C. J. Walker

Madam C. J. Walker is considered America's first self-made Black female millionaire. She had struggled with hair loss, so she created her own hair products, and once she saw that they worked well for her she started to sell them to help other Black women maintain healthy hair.

She not only made a name for herself, she also used business to empower Black women financially by employing them as Walker Agents. She created training schools and national conventions to help the women learn different sales strategies, learn more about the products, and celebrate the agents who went above and beyond. Madam Walker gave Black women a way to make a living other than working a low-paying job.

Madam Walker also gave back to the community by donating money to scholarships, homes for the elderly, anti-lynching efforts, and other initiatives within the local and national Black community. She extended her empire to the Caribbean and Latin America.[4]

The Netflix special based on her story is an inspiring look at what Madam Walker was able to accomplish, and Octavia Spencer does an amazing job of portraying her. In a time when Black women were only seen as the help, Madam Walker opened doors for Black women to be seen as successful entrepreneurs.

Eva Perón

Eva Perón, also known as Evita, was the first lady of Argentina from 1946 to 1952. She moved to Buenos Aires at the age of 15 to become an actress and ended co-owning a radio company. She was also one of the highest-paid radio actresses in the country.

She married Juan Perón, in 1945, and he was elected president the following year. Eva also helped Juan with his presidential campaign by delivering speeches on the radio and traveling with him around the country. She used her position as first lady to speak on behalf of labor rights and advocate for women's suffrage in Argentina. Here are some other notable achievements of Eva's:[5]

- She unofficially ran the Ministries of Labor and Health.
- She founded the Eva Perón Foundation to help those in need.
- She founded the nation's first large-scale female political party, the Female Peronist Party.

Health problems cut Eva's life short, but her contributions are still celebrated to this day through movies, books, plays, and a famous musical, *Evita*.

These are just a small number of women in history who made big moves to pave the way for all of us to become leaders in our own right.

More Women Are Needed in Leadership

There are proven benefits to having more women in leadership, including helping to solve big issues that women still face today. Here are some benefits that women leaders bring to different aspects of our culture.

Corporations

When women lead, everyone wins. An article from *Forbes* points out that companies with more women in board positions outperform those with fewer or no board positions held by women. It also leads to better profit margins for companies.

To see why we need more women in leadership roles in corporations, it's important to learn the buying power of women. The same article points out these facts:[6]

- According to *Harvard Business Review*, in 2009 women accounted for about $20 trillion in annual consumer expenditure.
- A decade later, women's spending power was reportedly around $31 trillion.
- Nielsen predicts that by 2028, women will own 75% of discretionary spending.

This is what corporations miss when they don't have more women in leadership roles. Women have tremendous buying power, so it makes sense to hire more women in these high corporate roles because women know how women spend money. If companies want to make a profit, then it's important to get the information from women. Companies lose revenue when they don't understand a woman's buying power.

The article also mentions that only 35% of creative advertising directors in the United States are women, which is a shockingly low number. Most corporations fail to recognize that in a marriage or partnership between a man and a woman, it's the woman who makes the buying decision, whether it's a car, a house, or even the vacuum cleaner. If companies better understood this concept, imagine the profit margins they would have.

Also, women have most of the qualities that would make them good leaders in the workplace. Consulting firm Hay Group published a study in 2016 that showed women surpass men in 11 of 12 major emotional intelligence characteristics, including emotional self-awareness, empathy, conflict management, flexibility, and teamwork.

If women in senior corporate roles are good for business, then why is the number of women represented in C-suite roles declining?

In 2023, women represented about 11.8% of senior corporate roles out of about 15,000 roles, a decrease from the previous year of 12.2%. One of the main reasons for this drop is that companies are focusing less on diversity, equity, and inclusion initiatives.[7]

Even in Fortune 500 companies, the representation of female CEOs is relatively small, even though research has found that companies have been more profitable with a female CEO. A study from the Frank Recruitment Group noted that 87% of Fortune 500 companies led by a female CEO have reported above-average profits, compared to the 78% of companies without a female CEO.[8] If this trend keeps decreasing, how are we going to achieve gender parity in the C-suite positions?

Here are some of the women CEOs of Fortune 500 companies who helped achieve above-average profits.

Karen S. Lynch, CVS   Karen Lynch has been the CEO of CVS Health Corporation since 2021 and has made some amazing achievements in such a short time, including bringing in record high revenues. In 2022, she helped the company bring in $322.5 billion in revenue, a 10.4% increase from $292.1 billion in 2021.[9] In 2023, CVS beat their revenue goals from the previous year by 10.9%, which amounted to $357.8 billion. CVS nearly doubled their profit margin within a year's time. The company made a profit of $4.3 billion in 2022 and $8.3 billion in 2023.[10] Lynch's leadership has helped CVS exceed their financial goals for each year she has been its CEO.

Lynch has also been recognized on:[11]

- *Forbes*'s inaugural "50 over 50" list
- The World's 100 Most Powerful Women in 2020 by *Forbes*
- Business Insider's Top 100 People Transforming Business list in 2019
- Fortune's list of the 50 Most Powerful Women in Business (2016–2020)

Priscilla Almodovar, Fannie Mae   Priscilla Almodovar has been the CEO of Fannie Mae since 2022. She is the first female CEO for the mortgage giant and she also made history as the first Latina CEO of a Fortune 500 company. That alone is already an achievement, and she has done wonders for Fannie Mae.

In 2023, home sales were at an all-time low due to low inventory, high prices, and high interest rates. Almodovar wanted to make home ownership accessible to everyone, and aimed to do so by acquiring about 805,000 single-family home loans, of which more than 45% were for first-time homebuyers. As a result, Fannie Mae ended up spending $369 billion into the housing market to help individuals and families buy, refinance, and rent approximately 1.5 million homes in 2023.[12]

Did that pay off for Fannie Mae? Yes it did. In 2023, Fannie Mae reported $77.4 billion in net worth, including $17.4 billion in additional net income for the full year. The net worth is a significant increase from previous years: $60.3 billion in 2022 and $47.4 billion in 2021.[13]

Thasunda Brown Duckett, TIAA   Thasunda Brown Duckett has been the CEO of financial services company TIAA since 2021, and she is one of only two Black female CEOs for a Fortune 500 Company. Duckett is passionate about bringing awareness to the racial retirement gap and the gender retirement gap.

In 2023, TIAA experienced record-high operating margins and the company now serves 400,000 individual participants with assets totaling $30 billion and nearly 500 institutions. Because of this asset growth, company revenue has tripled from two years ago.[14]

These are just a few of the women CEOs from Fortune 500 companies who are exceeding their financial goals. One thing I noticed about these women is their passion to help every individual have a chance at a great life, especially people in underserved groups. Whether it's helping them secure their first home or getting money for their retirement, their leadership resulted in an increase in revenue.

After seeing the data presented, how do we empower women and corporations to have more women in C-suite roles? A *Forbes* article shared 20 strategies from members of the Forbes Human Resources Council to help advance and keep women in the C-suite:[15]

- *Help women move past the "frozen middle."* Most women are stuck in the "frozen middle," and it's important to build leaders within your company. Create programs that will help women move past this stage and move up in the corporate ladder.
- *Encourage men to become active allies.* It is essential for men to support women in their corporate journey. When men are allies and support women to succeed, the performance of the company will also succeed.
- *Intentionally hire and coach women.* Companies must set clear intentions to include more women in C-suite roles and hire an executive coach to implement the intentions with success to avoid high turnover rates, which can be costly for companies.
- *Combat toxic narratives.* Imposter syndrome is something most women deal with, and it can stop them from stepping up. It's important for companies to create a safe space for women to share their struggles while helping them build their confidence. I have done speaking, workshops, and seminars for corporations on this topic to help women see their potential. Even the men get value out of it.
- *Establish supportive work policies.* It's essential for companies to create work policies that support women in their career and personal life. This support is without microaggressions or any passive-aggressive behaviors.
- *Offer mentorship programs.* It's important for women to know that they are not alone in this journey and providing mentorship

programs can be the solution. More experienced women in C-suite roles can guide up-and-coming women with their wisdom, knowledge, and experience to prepare them for the role.

- *Provide equal access to opportunity.* Actions speak louder than words, and while it's great that many companies value diversity and inclusion initiatives, they also have to act on them by providing the same access to tools and resources for women that their male colleagues receive.
- *Prioritize coaching and well-being.* Coaching is needed to help prioritize women's well-being in C-suite roles, and it will also help with retention rates. This is part of the personal and professional development for women to really succeed in their high-position roles.
- *Create networking opportunities.* Have an informal women's networking program by creating a social media–type forum where women can chat about anything. Have quarterly well-being events such as a book club discussion to create connections and build a supportive community.
- *Practice pay transparency.* Pay transparency benefits everyone in the company. By prioritizing pay transparency, companies take the necessary steps to make sure women are paid fairly for their work. The women will be happier because the company values their worth, and the company will benefit in the process.
- *Have senior leaders be advocates.* It's important that senior leaders also advocate to have more women in C-suite roles and continue to do so once they are in a C-suite role. Senior leaders can do this by mentoring women, including them in bigger projects, advocating for their promotion, and more.
- *Partner with strategic headhunters.* If you are working with a headhunter, partner with one who truly understands your worth and will advocate for you.
- *Promote an inclusive culture.* It's important for companies to create mentorship and sponsorship programs that address women's

unique career challenges and that support work-life balance. Providing flexible hours and promoting wellness initiatives will help women with job satisfaction and improve retention rates.

- *Ask what your women employees need.* Ask your employees with what they need support with. It may be remote work, mental health benefits, or even more mentorship. Find ways to deliver what they ask for. You can even have a suggestion box where employees can anonymously request something that is within reason.
- *Implement a "well-being scorecard."* Burnout is real and incorporating a well-being scorecard can help you evaluate the physical, mental, emotional, and social health of women. This can also help companies create mental well-being programs that will benefit all employees. It will cost companies more money if these programs are not implemented.
- *Give women a voice and an avenue.* Provide a platform where women feel seen and heard. This helps with retention rates and fosters a positive work environment. Figure out what will keep employees happy that goes beyond a salary and benefits.
- *Internally identify talented women.* Companies might not realize that the talent they are looking for is within their company. Check out women employees from all levels to see their leadership skills and/or leadership potential.
- *Create C-suite sponsorship programs.* I think this is a great idea where active C-suite members are also involved in this sponsorship program. In the program, active C-suite members can use their influence to actively open doors for women with leadership potential, openly advocate for their sponsored employee, and give opportunities to the sponsored employee that will gain exposure and advance within the company.
- *Make wellness part of your compensation package.* Investing in the well-being of any employee is essential. Lay out what dollar amount you will add to the psychological and well-being wages in the compensation package.

- *Treat everyone as human beings first.* This may sound silly but it is important that you treat people as human beings regardless of your position. Treating women as human beings will go a long way in your company and for the better.

By implementing some of these strategies, the results will be more women in C-suite roles and corporations will thrive in all areas.

Government

The current status of the representation of women in government positions is not the greatest. As of October 1, 2024, there are 29 countries with 30 women serving as heads of state and/or government. At this rate, it will take longer than 130 years to achieve gender parity.[16]

The representation of women in government is low, but there is proof that when women serve as heads of state and/or in government positions, the countries have flourished. A great example is during the COVID-19 lockdowns, when female-led countries were able to lessen the number of deaths. Here's are some details about that:

- *Jacinda Ardern.* The prime minister of New Zealand enforced strict lockdown rules as soon as the WHO declared COVID-19 a pandemic. She closed the borders to tourists even though tourism is one of the country's biggest industries. Because of her strict lockdowns, New Zealand was largely COVID free. The country had fewer than 2,500 COVID-19 fatalities and was known as having the lowest COVID-19 death rate in the Western world. Ardern was the global face for zero COVID, which was admired by many countries worldwide.[17]
- *Tsai Ing-wen.* As president of Taiwan, Tsai Ing-wen enforced strict lockdown rules for citizens, which paid off. Taiwan's residents were able to live a pretty normal life for most of 2020 while the rest of the world was in lockdown.

The country was considered a global success story at the height of the pandemic.[18]

- *Angela Merkel*. The chancellor of Germany also had strict lockdown measures, which resulted in low death rates. She had extensive testing measures, provided plenty of intensive-care beds, and set many reminders to take this lockdown seriously. Merkel also has a doctorate in quantum chemistry so she could clearly explain to the country the scientific reason why the lockdown was needed and most of the country approved of the lockdown because of it. Germany had one of the lowest COVID-19 death rates in the EU because of Merkel's measures.[19]

Of course, there were male-led countries that also saw some success stories from the pandemic, but few female-led countries did badly.

An article from the World Economic Forum also points out that countries where there is higher representation of females in government positions become more prosperous.[20]

One of the biggest benefits to having more women in government is the removal of laws that hurt women's equality. This is definitely an important one because there are so many countries where women cannot even go to school or get a job. And when women have the opportunity to work and earn money, this also benefits the country as a whole. GDP increases as well.

The removal of such laws also scores higher on the World Bank's Women, Business, and the Law (WBL) Index, which determines the legal equality of economic opportunity. If a country gets a score of 100, this means that their laws protect the rights off all citizens. Unfortunately, there are only 14 countries that have a score of 100:

Belgium

Canada

Denmark

France

Germany

Greece

Iceland

Ireland

Latvia

Luxembourg

Netherlands

Portugal

Spain

Sweden

I am proud to see Canada on this list and quite surprised that the United States is not on it, especially when there is so much pride saying that they are the Land of the Free. Since only 14 countries have a perfect score, we are left with 2.4 billion women worldwide who do not live in countries with full legal protections and opportunities. They do not have the equal opportunity to succeed.

It's important that every country has more women elected in office because they have the power to eliminate laws that hurt women. When there are more laws that give women the opportunity to work and make a living for themselves, the nation prospers. Currently, the female workforce participation is 30% lower than male participation worldwide. If each country had full female participation, the global GDP would increase by 20%.[21]

There has been some progress but it's still at a very slow pace and at the rate we are going, it's going to take more than 130 years to achieve gender parity. So if we know that having more women in government is a necessity, how do we make this happen?

The United Nations Development Programme (UNDP) did a study on elevating women's roles in politics in Ukraine and provided the following solutions:[22]

- *Quotas.* The study found that during Ukraine's 2020 elections, women were actively participating in politics due to the fact that Ukraine legally imposed a gender quota to ensure gender balance from political parties. When a certain political party was able to meet the quota, they also received additional funding to finance their statutory activities, and also were encouraged to involve women in politics.
- *Gender policy of political parties.* To ensure that gender balance is achieved in Ukraine's political parties, a gender audit is conducted. By conducting the gender audit, parties see where there are opportunities available for women to be in government roles and show how women can create a positive impact for the political party. The audit also helps create programs for women to level up and be more visible.
- *Inter-factional associations and groups.* Like any other industry, Ukraine's government is often seen as a "man's world," which is why it's important to have groups and/or associations where women are seen and heard. Having groups like these means there is mutual respect and support for creating gender equality solutions.
- *Mentoring.* Self-doubt and negative stereotypes may stop women from entering politics. Mentorship is essential so that women can improve their skills, increase their confidence, and gain experience as well. Having political party mentorship programs can help women realize their potential and step up as leaders.
- *Training and leadership programs for women.* Providing these kinds of programs for women in office and for women who are thinking of entering politics teaches women different skills that will be prepare them to become successful in politics.

Recently I came across some posts on X where women from Afghanistan shared videos of themselves singing out loud. To you it may just be a video of a woman singing, but in Afghanistan it is a different story. The Taliban had just prohibited women from speaking or showing their face in public, because they believe that women's voices and bodies lead men into temptation and vice. Women aren't allowed to sing or read aloud even inside their own homes.[23]

This is why women from Afghanistan are singing aloud in their videos. Even though they are still covered, they are singing as a way to fight this law created by the Taliban. This is more than a human rights issue; this is erasing women's freedom to be themselves and this is why we need more women in government positions. It's important for us to cancel laws like this to save the women from extreme groups like the Taliban.

It is clear that having more women in government positions will help save the world and yes, this may sound bold, but after reading the stories and the positive outcomes, I truly believe this is the solution that will benefit everyone.

Entrepreneurship

Women entrepreneurs have been on a fast pace since the pandemic and beyond. Women are starting businesses at a higher rate than men, which in turn is fueling the economy. A 2024 report from Wells Fargo shared the following information:[24]

- Women-owned businesses in the United States represent 39.1% of all businesses (which total over 14 million businesses), and employ 12.2 million workers, generating $2.7 trillion.
- The number of women-owned businesses between 2019 and 2023 increased at nearly double the rate of those owned by men.
- Even though the COVID-19 lockdowns led to many business closures, women actually launched more businesses than they closed. The number of men opening businesses during the pandemic declined.

- Women-owned businesses provided jobs and created more revenue during the pandemic while revenue of men's businesses declined.
- From 2019 to 2023, the growth rate of women-owned businesses outpaced the rate of men at 94.3% for number of firms, 252.8% for employment, and 82.0% for revenue.
- During the pandemic, women-owned businesses added 1.4 million jobs and $579.6 billion in revenue to the economy.
- Nearly half a million women-owned businesses with revenues between $250,000 and $999,999 grew their aggregate revenues by about 30%, illustrating their ambition, grit, and readiness to cross the $1 million revenue threshold.

What do these facts tell you? I think it says a lot of things. After reading this report, this is what I can say about women-owned businesses:

- When faced with a huge crisis, women entrepreneurs succeeded during one of the most trying times of the world.
- Women-owned businesses contributed more money to the economy and employed people with more jobs.
- Women succeeded because of their resiliency to thrive when given the right tools and resources, such as government aid, bank loans, and the like.

Even though these numbers are encouraging, there is still a lot of work to do. While women-owned businesses do represent 39.1% of all businesses in the United States, they only account for 9.2% of the workforce and 5.8% of revenue.

How can almost 40% of women-owned businesses in America only account for less than 6% of the revenue? If women-owned businesses had the proper tools and resources to really succeed, the United States has the potential to generate $7.9 trillion in additional revenue. This is why it's important to close the gap between men- and women-owned businesses.

Here are five challenges faced by women entrepreneurs and how to tackle these challenges:[25]

1. Work-Life Balance

Women are not only entrepreneurs; women are the cooks, the tutors, the caregivers, the ones who have to run errands, plan meals, and so much more. Women have to do it all, so there is very little time left to dedicate to their business. Women face not only business challenges but also everyday challenges in the household. To be honest, I don't think there is such a thing as a work-life balance because life is chaotic and when you are a woman who is trying to do it all, you do the best you can and try to find time to squeeze in everything possible.

To achieve this so-called balance is to learn to ask for help from your spouse or other family members so you have more time to concentrate on your business. It's time to eliminate this notion that you have to be the "superwoman" for everyone. If you have the funds to hire people to do certain things, invest in it because your ROI will be better. If you do not have the funds to hire help, do a barter trade with someone or bring in students who are looking for internships. It is okay to ask and receive help as much as possible.

I know this isn't always easy because we feel ashamed for seeking support, but let that idea go. The help you receive will be better for everyone in the long run and your business will do better because of it. Another thing that needs to be done is to set boundaries, which can be uncomfortable but is necessary to get the results we desire. Start setting boundaries around you so you can focus on figuring out how to bring more cashflow into your business.

Ultimately, I think it's important to get rid of this work-life balance notion. I feel like women are trying to attain something that is unattainable. When men focus on their business, they may have 12–14 hours (or more) a day to make it work, and they have the luxury to do that because they have fewer responsibilities, because they probably have women in their lives who run the household in the background.

When people ask me how to achieve work-life balance, my answer is usually, "I don't know how that is possible."

And I say that because I don't even know what that balance looks like. Everyone has different lives to live, different routines, different paths, so everyone's outlook on life looks different. If you think work-life balance is about 50/50, then I think many people will fail because not everyone can achieve that. So this is why I think work-life balance is a myth that needs to be dismantled.

2. Burnout

Burnout is a real thing, especially for women. As I mentioned before, women aren't thinking only about their business. They're also thinking about their children, their parents, their household, and other things. It's rare that a man has to go through that.

And because a woman tries to do everything herself, she gets exhausted and burnt out that much faster. We saw that during the COVID-19 lockdowns, when women were not only working on their business and/or job, but were also homeschooling their children, doing household chores, and attending to their immediate family. It can take a toll on us trying to do everything ourselves. The worst part about this is that women are expected to do this while men do not have the same expectations placed on them.

It's important to incorporate a self-care routine so that you can take time to yourself to have some breathing room. I have a whole chapter on self-love and self-care from my previous book, *The Tao of Self-Confidence*.

3. Lack of Support

Women entrepreneurs crave support but are afraid to ask for it and the journey of becoming an entrepreneur can be a very lonely one. Feeling alone in this journey can take a toll on your confidence, and you end up not taking action. This is why it's important to have support groups, masterminds, and mentorships available to women entrepreneurs.

Men seek support all the time. You see this brotherhood they have created through mastermind groups and more. This is one of the reasons that men are able to succeed faster than women, because they don't do it alone.

Start looking for groups and networking opportunities that can give you the support you need in your entrepreneurship journey. I am very fortunate that I have joined masterminds and groups that can help me see what is stopping me from moving forward and give me different solutions that I can utilize in my own business. Start searching the internet or ask your sphere of influence if there are support groups out there that you can be part of. You can also join our community Tao Queens for support — https://facebook.com/groups/taoqueens.

4. Prejudice and Bias

Of course women are rarely taken seriously in business, and because of that we tend to resist taking action. Women are up against so many biases, it can bring their spirits down. It can be really frustrating when you see men getting funding just by writing an idea on a napkin while you have a whole presentation done and you still get rejected.

These biases and prejudice are there no matter what we do, which is why it's important to cut out the noise and remember why you decided to become an entrepreneur. As a woman, you will have to work so much harder than a man and that is the hard truth, but it's also worth it when you can break barriers and open the doors for so many other women.

Addressing prejudice and bias is not easy, and it can be complicated because there are certain laws that don't help women entrepreneurs at all (and why we need more women in government). This is why it's important to connect with people who have the power to create the necessary changes. It can be someone in public office who can change policies that will benefit women entrepreneurs or another entrepreneur who can create the change you seek. You don't have to address this issue by yourself. This change will take time, but if we keep on moving forward by showing up together, we can combat this.

It has to start with ourselves getting clear as to why we started a business and take ourselves seriously so that others can see that you mean business. This journey will have more downs than ups, but it will be worth the ride.

5. Financing for Women Entrepreneurs

It's no secret that women entrepreneurs receive fewer funding options than men. Most women are either self-funding their business or have to ask for a loan from family members. Even trying to get a bank loan isn't a walk in the park. The value of bank loans women entrepreneurs receive is less than what men receive due to the bias and prejudice that still affects us today.

A report from Lendio (a small business finance provider) shared the following stats about women entrepreneurs and financing:[26]

- 25% of women are denied a business loan versus 19% of men.
- Women-owned businesses received just 32.6% of the approvals and 28.4% of the dollars offered in SBA 7(a) (Small Business Advisory primary business loan program) and 504 (fixed-rated, long-term loans for small businesses) loans in the 2023 fiscal year.

o Women are less likely to receive the full amount of funds requested. In 2023, 45% of women-owned businesses were fully approved for the loan requested versus 55% of men-owned businesses.

o 38% of women-owned businesses are operating at a profit versus 47% of men-owned businesses.

o 33% of men-owned businesses have annual revenues of $1 million or more versus 16% of women-owned businesses.

Other factors include women receiving lower amounts in bank loans and paying higher interest rates if they do receive a bank loan.

It's important to eliminate the gender funding gap that women still face today by creating equal opportunity for women to gain financing for their businesses. With these restrictions, this can make or break a woman's business.

The Need for More Women Billionaires

It's great to know that we have reached a record high when it comes to the number of female billionaires in the world, but that number is still a fraction of male billionaires in the world.

Forbes released their list of the richest self-made women in 2024. Out of 2,781 billionaires listed, only 369 of them are female. This means that about 13% of billionaires are women and collectively they are worth nearly $1.8 trillion, which is a $240 billion increase from 2023.[27] If you compare this to men's net worth, theirs is about $12.4 trillion, which means there is a huge wealth gap between men and women.[28]

Another *Forbes* article mentioned that out of the 369 women who are billionaires, only 3.6% of them are self-made. Yet even though the number of self-made women billionaires is small, it's almost four times higher than a decade ago, with most of these women billionaires coming from China and the United States.

It's sad to know this gap exists in 2024 but I am happy to know that more women billionaires are showing up and slowly climbing the charts. We definitely need to see more of that, and I love that the list also has some women who are newcomers into the billionaire club, 15 newcomers to be exact. Women like Taylor Swift, Lisa Su, and Rihanna are some of the self-made billionaire newcomers.[29]

After seeing these numbers, it's imperative that we find ways to close the gender wealth gap, and I know that it's a battle because women still go through so many barriers that stop us from getting to the top. I also know that when women have the financial means, they are more willing to spend their wealth for unselfish reasons like helping the needy.

MacKenzie Scott is a prime of example of a woman who gives back. She has donated over $16 billion since 2019 and continues to give back. Scott mentioned that she is giving away half of her net worth to philanthropic efforts. In March 2024, she opened a process for groups to apply for funding, providing $1 million grants to 250 organizations.[30]

Taylor Swift is another billionaire who gives back. During her Eras Tour, she gave $55 million in bonuses to every person who worked on her tour, and I mean every single person from the backup dancers to the truckers to the caterers and more.[31] Swift has also donated to many other charitable organizations. Here are some notable additional donations Swift made through the years.[32]

> August 2016—Swift donated money to the doctors and the team who saved her godson's life. In the same year she also donated $1 million to Louisiana flood relief.

> August 2017—Swift made a donation to actress Mariska Hargitay's Joyful Heart Foundation that focuses on helping sexual assault survivors.

> March 2020—Swift donated $1 million to the Nashville tornado relief efforts that killed at least 24 people and

destroyed many homes. In the same month, she also made donations to fans who were struggling with the COVID-19 crisis.

December 2023—Swift donated $1 million to the Community Foundation of Middle Tennessee after tornadoes affected many people and damaged many buildings.

February 2024—Swift donated $100,000 to a GoFundMe campaign of the family of a radio DJ who was killed during the Kansas City Chiefs victory parade.

And according to the Women's Philanthropy Institute at the Indiana University Lilly Family School of Philanthropy, women with income in the top percentiles donated 156% more to charities than men. The biggest reason for this is that women are more selfless and find ways to promote social change, while men tend to donate money to charities for reasons of self-interest or to maintain the status quo.[33]

A great example of a man who donated to charity for personal interest is Elon Musk, the second richest person in the world. Since 2020, he has donated $7 billion to charity. What most people don't realize is that he donated that money to his own foundation as a way to get enormous tax breaks.[34]

It's clear that when women have financial wealth, they are more willing to give back and they are passionate about creating a positive impact in the world. Imagine how much more positive impact the world would have if we built up more women billionaires. We need more women in leadership roles in all industries because everyone benefits.

I hope this chapter was eye-opening for you and you can start applying the suggestions to start your leadership journey. In the next and final chapter, I will be talking about the formula for women's leadership.

8

Ready, Fire, Aim: The Formula for Women's Leadership

I CAN'T BELIEVE this is the last chapter! We've covered so many important things throughout this book and this chapter is just as important.

If you want to learn how to become a leader, you need to learn the formula to do it:

Ready, Fire, Aim

Yes, you read that right. We've all heard "Ready, aim, fire." But the correct formula is actually "Ready, fire, aim."

To get the results that we want, we have to go out there and be okay with making mistakes because we learn from them how to make things better. We have to keep taking action and course-correct along the way to get to our desired results. Leadership isn't about being perfect—far from it. It's learning along the way as you continue to take action.

I wouldn't be here today if it weren't for the mistakes I've made along the way. I know that the idea of making mistakes can be scary, especially for a woman. I still get scared of making mistakes because I fear that other people will think I'm a fraud or a failure. But I also realize that mistakes will happen and it's a sign that you are taking action in your journey.

In fact, I've come to realize that mistakes can present some of your greatest possibilities because they can lead you to the right opportunities you've been seeking all your life. Leaders make mistakes all the time, and I want you to realize that so you can go out there and make magic.

There were times when people told me where I went wrong. At first I would feel so bad that I made those mistakes that I delayed my own success or resisted taking action. Now I recognize that I only know what I only know. And even though I made those mistakes (and still make mistakes), I still achieved writing two books in two years for Wiley (which is one of the largest publishing companies in the world), making the *Wall Street Journal* bestseller list, having a podcast in the 0.5% most popular shows in the world, and so much more. This is why I am so grateful for the mistakes I've made because I would not have achieved what I have if I hadn't made them or had stopped what I was doing after making them.

And you think men have it figured out? Far from it. Even the so called "gurus" you see in the media are figuring it out as they go. They still make a ton of mistakes but they move forward anyway. I know it can be easier for guys to make mistakes and not get criticized because they are men. Women get criticized much more than men do, but the only real mistake we make is if it stops us from moving forward. This is why you have to learn to work past those mistakes and any criticism that may come from them, because for leaders that's part of the process. When you learn to tune out the noise and focus on your mission, you become unstoppable.

When I was approached by Wiley to write my first solo book, I really had no clue what I was going to write about. I had never written a full book on my own, and I had less than three months to write it so it could be launched in May 2023 for AAPI Heritage Month. All I had was an outline that I presented to the publisher and got the green light. The next day I started my writing journey and figured it out along the way. Sometimes I sat in Starbucks staring at the computer screen for hours, trying to figure out what I was going to write.

So I started searching for related topics, writing down my own stories, and even watching movies so I could figure out what content I wanted to cover. The manuscript was all over the place but I was able to write the book in record time. I'm still in shock that I was able to get it finished in such a short time, but I'm really glad I managed to make it happen, despite having had no clue where to start.

I recently watched the movie *Space Cadet*, in which Emma Roberts plays a bartender accidentally accepted into the NASA space program. As a kid, it was her dream to be an astronaut but life got in the way and she became a bartender instead. When she sees one of her schoolmates make a name for himself, she decides to go back and figure out how to be an astronaut and begins by applying for the NASA program and putting together her resume. She asks her best friend to make her resume look more professional, but instead the best friend lies on the resume and Roberts's character gets accepted into the NASA program. From then on, she figures out the mental and physical exercises she must accomplish to be accepted as an astronaut.

Now I'm not saying you should lie on your resume—you definitely should not. The character in that movie didn't realize it was a lie, but once she was already in that position, instead of quitting she was determined to find a way to live her dream as an astronaut. Even if she failed, at least she went for it and she would live with no regrets. Men often put themselves in situations where they have no clue what to do but realize that they have a shot, and they will take that shot regardless of the possible outcome.

I want to share some lessons that will help you with the Ready, Fire, Aim formula for leadership, to go out there, make mistakes, and course-correct along the way.

Be Unconventional

Sometimes you have to do things outside the norm. People are successful because they did things differently and thought out of the box. The unconventional road can be lonely at times but it has also created so many things that were once thought impossible. My journey is totally unconventional in my culture, which dictates that I am supposed to get married, have kids, and live a traditional life. Starting a podcast, becoming a speaker, and writing a book is completely outside the Asian culture playbook but I went for it anyway, because I believed it was necessary to create better representation for Asian women, and by extension to create better representation for all women. Have the courage to be unconventional and dare to do things differently. That's how legends are made.

Realize Your Potential

Part of the reason why you are stuck where you are is because you don't realize your potential. So much untapped potential is waiting for you to create the magic that you were meant to do on this planet. But the way you perceive yourself is stopping you from getting there. The only way you can realize it is if you believe in yourself, believe in your capabilities, and just go out there and take action. Yes, mistakes will be made, but what you accomplish will surprise you.

Shoot Your Shot

You've probably heard this famous quote by Michael Jordan: "You miss 100 percent of the shots you don't take!"

This is so true. Part of the reason you may not take that shot is that you're afraid of rejection and/or failure. We constantly see rejection and failure as the end of all ends, not recognizing that it is part of the process. If you continue not to shoot your shot, nothing happens either, guaranteed. Here's something else Michael Jordan shared that helped him become one of the greatest basketball players of all time:

I've missed more than 9,000 shots in my career. I've lost almost 300 games. Twenty-six times I've been trusted to take the game-winning shot and missed. I've failed over and over and over again in my life. And that is why I succeed.

He succeeded because he had to miss shots and lose games. He didn't get up and became a pro-athlete overnight. It took all the missed shots and losses to get him to his success. Many successful people, have to go through so much loss in order to gain their success, but they often avoid talking about their failures or the real story behind their success. The overnight success you see on social media is really due to years of hard work, failure, mistakes, rejections, ugly crying, and a belief that they can make it happen. It all starts with shooting your shot.

Take that Second Chance

So many people think they have lost their chance to do great things or to live life on their terms. I want you to realize that you can have a second chance at life. I have seen so many people who started their careers in their 40s or older, went back to school, and finished something they started 10 years ago, all because they realized they could take a second chance at life. Maybe you wanted to be a model but you think you are too old to be one. That is a total myth. Many seniors have made a name for themselves by showcasing their outfits on Instagram and created a career out of it. It's important to realize that your chance isn't gone. As long as you are still breathing here on this earth, you can still do something to change the course of your life.

Create a New Normal

It's important for us as leaders to create a new normal so we can realize the positive changes we want to see in this world. We must learn to push through the biases and find new ways of solving problems to get there. Think about how many companies created a new normal for our society. We have cars that we can plug in and charge, phones that take high-quality videos, and more. None of that would have happened if people hadn't had the vision to create a new normal. So think about what a new normal looks like for you. Do you want more women to be seen as leaders, give them equal opportunity, and take down all of the biases women still face today? Start figuring out how you will be able to make that happen.

Make the Impossible Possible

There are so many examples in the world where we made the impossible possible by taking action. Think about how many women have broken barriers and opened the doors for other women: women who have won gold medals, become billionaires, become heads of state, and more, all because they believe in themselves and in their capabilities to make it happen no matter what challenges may come their way. It may seem impossible at times but when you work toward making it possible, you surprise yourself and what you are capable of. Impossible is really "I'm possible!"

Understand that a Little Embarrassment or Failure Won't Kill You, but Giving Up Will

Yes, you will fail and maybe be a little bit embarrassed at times during this journey. I've had many of these moments. But here's the real deal: it's temporary. When you give up on your dreams, that is long lasting and will haunt you for the rest of your life. So many people give up when they are three feet from gold. If you believe in yourself, your mission, and what you can accomplish, then know that feeling a little bit of embarrassment or failure is just part of the process. One of my biggest fears is to look back and regret the things I gave up on, which is why I keep moving forward. I can honestly say that I have no regrets in life because I was able to achieve everything I ever wanted to do. I have met so many people who were totally miserable with their life because they gave up too quickly. That's not what I want for you!

Remember That You Gotta Have Grit

Leadership isn't short-term, and it may take years to get where you're going. Are you willing to keep moving forward? Having grit in your journey is so important because many challenges and road-blocks will come your way. If you continue to persevere and weather the storms, you will get there. Yes, this journey can bring us down at times, and you may question whether you are on the right path. But if you know where you're going in the end, you will stubbornly find ways to get there.

Take a Chance on Yourself

Be willing to bet on yourself. Your biggest cheerleader in life is *you*. If you don't take a chance on yourself, how do you expect others to take a chance on you? Part of the reason I have been able to attract the opportunities I wanted is because I decided to bet on myself and show others my capabilities. It can be hard at times because you feel you have to prove your worth to others. I still feel like I need others' approval to be seen as successful or as worthy. I have to remind myself that I am more than enough and be willing to take a chance on myself to do great things. When you learn to take a chance on yourself, you will be surprised at what you can accomplish.

Keep Showing Up

It's important to show up even if you think nobody is listening. When I first started my podcast, I had no influence. I had no clue if anyone was listening to what I was saying or if anybody knew I was there, but I kept showing up because I believed that people needed to see and hear these stories. As the years went by, so many people messaged me to say how they have been a fan of my podcast for so long. Just because you think nobody is paying attention, it doesn't mean you stop showing up. People may be watching what you're doing and cheering for you in silence. This is why it's impor-tant to show up as much as you can because the more you show up, the more people will see what you're doing and be silently rooting for you. You may have to show up even when you're the only person in the room. That's okay, that's life and it's just practice on your end. Don't let the disappointing moments stop you from showing up for yourself and for others.

The Future of Women's Leadership

This world is ever evolving, and now with the rise of AI, it's important for women to utilize this technology for good. I currently have very little knowledge of AI (I even had to look up what "prompt" meant in AI terms), but that doesn't mean I cannot learn it or team up with the right people who will use this technology for good.

In fact, at the beginning of this book, I mentioned to you about partnering with the coach of coaches, Mark Anthony Bates, and creating the Tao Queens and Queen Makers programs that will help women harness their power to become leaders or "queens" in their respective industries.

When AI first came onto the scene, I was totally against it because I thought it would take away jobs. I was running on a scarcity mindset. Instead of hating AI, I had to learn to embrace it because this technology is here to stay. Right now we are also facing a gender gap in AI, which means that if women don't learn this technology sooner rather than later, we end up on the losing end again.

The World Economic Forum stated that an AI-driven future is a way to have more women in leadership roles. Generative AI is transforming the workplace where three out of four desk-based roles now use it in their jobs. New technology means learning new skills, and if we don't learn this new technology in our jobs and/or businesses, women end up losing out again, and so does the economy.[1] Learning how to use AI is essential for every woman to live better lives, become better leaders, and bring more wealth to women.

Last summer, Mark Anthony and his team in Singapore reached out to me asking if I wanted to collaborate on making the Tao

Queens and Queen Maker programs. To be honest, I was hesitant at first to partner with them because I was still wondering if I was capable enough to do it. But then I remembered the question that Mark Anthony asked me, which appears at the beginning of this book:

Are you ready to level up this year, or are you okay with all the mediocrity that you have currently?

I told Mark Anthony I was ready to level up, and even though I didn't know what I was getting into, I said yes because I knew the outcome was going to make a positive impact for women globally. Mark Anthony and the team have big hearts to help women succeed, and that is also why I decided to partner with them. Their values align with mine and that is so important for me.

And what do the Tao Queens and Queens Makers consist of? These are the tools and resources that will help you become a leader or "queen" in your respective field. Key elements of the program include:

Empowerment and leadership. Encouraging women to step into leadership roles and influence their surroundings positively

Skill development. Offering training and resources to build business acumen, marketing skills, and technological proficiency

Mindset shift. Focusing on changing limiting beliefs and developing a success-oriented mindset

Support system. Creating a community of like-minded women who support and uplift each other

Digital tools and AI. Utilizing AI and digital platforms to provide coaching, advice, and business development resources accessible anytime

Recognition and celebration. Highlighting and rewarding the achievements of women in the program through events and awards

And this is more than a program; this is a tribe of Queens who will create a ripple effect where empowered women can influence and assist others in their communities, fostering a network of strong, confident leaders. I am really excited about this next chapter in my life because this is a brand-new thing for me and while it can be scary, it is also exciting, and I do hope you become part of this tribe. To solve the big issues women still face today, we have to work together to create a better tomorrow.

And because you have read this book to the end, I wanted to give you something as a token of appreciation. You can download free resources at https://taoqueens.com/gift that will help you with the mindset to unleash the inner Queen in you.

Being a leader isn't always easy, especially as a woman. With great power comes great responsibility. I know that sounds cheesy but this is the hard truth. It's truly important that we take our leadership position seriously because, unfortunately, when one woman screws up, we all pay for it.

I am not saying that you have to be the "perfect" leader to show up, but I do believe that you can't take this position lightly. You have to take yourself seriously so that others will treat you with the respect you deserve. If we want gender parity to be achieved in less than 130 years, then we have to start putting in the work. Women will have to work 10, 100, or even 1,000 times harder to make this happen. It won't be an easy thing to do, but together it is possible! Let's continue to show the world what women are truly capable of.

Our younger generation needs more roles models like you, and I want you to show them what is possible.

Conclusion

CONFIDENCE AND LEADERSHIP are a never-ending journey. You will learn new things every single day and face challenges ahead. The most important part is that you have the tools and resources to help you get there, and if you don't, the Tao Queens and Queen Maker programs are there for you.

As women, we still face many biases and a gender gap, but I also believe that we can create so many opportunities because of it. These gaps are also a sign that we have the opportunity to create something that will leave a lasting positive impact, not just for women but for the whole world.

I truly believe that women are the solution to the current problems happening around the world. There is proof that having more women in leadership leads to win-win situations for everyone, especially when they can reach their full potential. The more women can show up and show other women what is possible, the more I believe gender parity will take less than 130 years to achieve.

We have to work together to make this happen. Women are stronger in numbers, and when we can work together toward a better future, we become invincible. This is our time to shine.

We have been hiding in the background for far too long. Hiding who we truly are and what we are capable of is doing a disservice to the world.

If you want to get the most out of this book, I suggest you read it more than one time and highlight the lessons that stand out to you the most. The more you implement the actions in the book, the better it will be for you. Make sure to apply what you have learned because that is how you start getting the results. Also, sign up for the free resources from Tao Queens (https://taoqueens.com) and Queen Makers (https://queenmaker.ai) to help you get a jump start.

I really appreciate you for staying until the end. Writing this book has been an amazing journey for me, as well as showing me what women all over the world are really going through. We may not come from the same culture but I know we still go through similar situations and face many of the same barriers. Let's combine forces to break down those barriers.

And I want to end with this quote from feminist poet and illustrator Rupi Kaur:

> "What's the greatest lesson a woman should learn? That since day one, she's already had everything she needs within herself. It's the world that convinced her she did not."

You got this, and always know that I am rooting for you, Queen!

Notes

Introduction

1. World Economic Forum, "Global Gender Gap Report 2023," n.d., https://www.weforum.org/publications/global-gender-gap-report-2023/infographics-66115127a8.
2. Anna Tabitha Bonfert and Divyanshi Wadhwa, "International Women's Day 2024: Five Insightful Charts on Gender (in)Equality Around the World," World Bank Blogs (blog), March 16, 2024, https://blogs.worldbank.org/en/opendata/international-womens-day-2024-five-insightful-charts-gender-inequality-around-world.

Chapter 1

1. Monika, "46 Examples of Double Standards in Our Society That You're Probably Guilty Of," Bored Panda, August 4, 2017, https://www.boredpanda.com/double-standards-comic-illustrations.
2. Emily Burack, "Read America Ferrera's Powerful Monologue in Barbie," *Town & Country*, August 5, 2023, https://www.townandcountrymag.com/leisure/arts-and-culture/a44725030/america-ferrera-barbie-full-monologue-transcript.

3. Maree Corbo and Amanda Alford, "The Shockingly High Rate of Violence Against Indigenous Women Shows the Long Tail of Colonisation," *The Guardian*, January 24, 2024, https://www.theguardian.com/commentisfree/2024/jan/25/the-shockingly-high-rates-of-violence-against-indigenous-women-demonstrates-the-long-tail-of-colonisation.

4. Jillian Horton, "Op Ed: The Firestorm over the Firing of a Gray-Haired Female News Anchor in Canada," *Los Angeles Times*, September 2, 2022, https://www.latimes.com/opinion/story/2022-09-02/lisa-laflamme-gray-hair-women-workplace.

5. National Organization for Women, "Get the Facts," n.d., https://now.org/now-foundation/love-your-body/love-your-body-whats-it-all-about/get-the-facts.

6. Jannik Lindner, "The Most Surprising Body Shaming Statistics in 2024," Gitnux, May 27, 2024, https://gitnux.org/body-shaming-statistics.

7. Straits Research, "The Global Skin Lightening Products Market Size Is Predicted to Reach at USD 16.08 billion by 2030, Increasing at a CAGR of 5.56%," January 10, 2024, https://finance.yahoo.com/news/global-skin-lightening-products-market-133000572.html.

8. Kathleen Magramo, "First Black Filipino Woman Crowned as Miss Universe Philippines," CNN, May 24, 2024, https://www.cnn.com/2024/05/24/style/chelsea-manalo-miss-universe-philippines-intl-hnk/index.html.

9. Sreshtha Roychowdhury, "'I Get the Rabbit Food Question?': Robert Downey Jr. Shut Down Subtle Sexist Question Fired at Scarlett," *FandomWire*, March 29, 2024, https://fandomwire.com/i-get-the-rabbit-food-question-robert-downey-jr-shut-down-subtle-sexist-question-fired-at-scarlett-johansson-with-witty-reply-to-defend-avengers-co-star.

10. https://www.facebook.com/watch/?extid=SEO----&v=495528628254543

11. Women in the World, "WITW L.A. Salon: Viola Davis on Being Told She's 'a Black Meryl Streep,'" February 14, 2018, https://www.youtube.com/watch?v=Sf0kDGVkVzQ.

12. Katherine Haan, "Gender Pay Gap Statistics in 2024," Forbes Advisor, March 1, 2024, https://www.forbes.com/advisor/business/gender-pay-gap-statistics.

13. Monique Woodard, "Unlocking the trillion-dollar female economy," TechCrunch, May 21, 2023, https://techcrunch.com/2023/05/21/unlocking-the-trillion-dollar-female-economy.

14. Ilyse Liffreing, "What Brands Can Learn From Stanley and the Buying Power of Women," The Current, March 7, 2024, https://www.thecurrent.com/stanely-brands-women-advertising.

15. Ivana Pino, "The Motherhood Penalty, Explained," Fortune Recommends, June 14, 2024, https://fortune.com/recommends/banking/the-motherhood-penalty.

16. Henadi Al-Saleh, "Empowering Female Founders: How We Can Narrow the Gender Gap in Venture Capital," World Economic Forum, December 28, 2023, https://www.weforum.org/agenda/2023/12/how-we-can-close-the-venture-capital-gender-gap.

17. Sam Blum, "Adam Neumann's Mysterious Real Estate Startup, Flow, Has a $300 Million Plan For Miami," *Inc.*, March 19, 2024, https://www.inc.com/sam-blum/adam-neumanns-mysterious-real-estate-startup-flow-has-a-300-million-plan-for-miami.html

18. Sarah Benstead, "'Bro Culture': What Is It and Why It's Still an Issue," Breathe blog, January 5, 2024, https://www.breathehr.com/en-gb/blog/topic/company-culture/bro-culture-and-why-its-an-issue-for-startups.

19. Christine Shen, "Today, I filed a lawsuit against my former employer. I believe I was drugged at a work event, and after. . .," LinkedIn, February 27, 2024, https://www.linkedin.com/posts/christine-shen-2494777_womeninbusiness-nytimes-activity-7168336984225120257-3kuF?utm_source=share&utm_medium=member_desktop.

20. Women in Tech Network, "Women in Tech Stats 2024," n.d., https://www.womentech.net/en-us/women-in-tech-stats.

21. Emily Rella, "'Wildly Inappropriate': Woman Says She Was Denied a Job Because She Didn't Wear Makeup During the Interview," *Entrepreneur*, March 27, 2024, https://www.entrepreneur.com/business-news/recruiter-rejects-woman-from-vp-job-for-not-wearing-makeup/471771.

22. Mike Wendling, "Ghislaine Maxwell Appeals Sex Abuse Conviction," BBC, March 12, 2024, https://www.bbc.com/news/world-us-canada-68515516.

23. Tommy McArdle and Dory Jackson, "Mira Sorvino Tears up at 90s Con While Recalling How Harvey Weinstein 'Stifled' Her Career," *People*, March 18, 2024.

24. Plan Street, "Quick Facts About Sexual Assault in America – 2024," March 25, 2022, https://www.planstreetinc.com/quick-facts-about-sexual-assault-in-america.

25. Nour Ghantous, "3 Countries Where Sharia Law Is Hardest on Women," *FairPlanet*, August 31, 2023, https://www.fairplanet.org/story/3-countries-where-sharia-law-is-hardest-on-women.

26. Amnesty International, "Iran: Security Forces Used Rape and Other Sexual Violence to Crush 'Woman Life Freedom' Uprising with Impunity," December 6, 2023, https://www.amnesty.org/en/latest/news/2023/12/iran-security-forces-used-rape-and-other-sexual-violence-to-crush-woman-life-freedom-uprising-with-impunity.

27. Antonio Graceffo, "The Genocidal Islamic State Almost Wiped Out the Yazidis. They Are still Suffering," Mercator, February 19, 2024, https://www.mercatornet.com/the_genocidal_islamic_state_almost_wiped_the_yazidis.

28. "Islamic Sharia Law," https://www.billionbibles.org/sharia/sharia-law.html.

29. Imtiaz Tyab, "Taliban Vows to Ensure Women's Rights Under Islamic Sharia Law. What Does That Mean?," *CBS News*, August 20, 2021, https://www.cbsnews.com/news/afghanistan-islamic-sharia-law-womens-rights-what-is.

30. Denzil, "Influence of religion on women's rights." Discovering Belgium, February 18, 2024, https://www.discoveringbelgium.com/influence-of-religion-on-womens-rights/.

31. Nick Robertson, "'Smallville' Actress Sentenced in NXIVM Cult Sex-Trafficking Case Secures Early Release from Prison," The Hill Blog Briefing Room, July 5, 2023, https://thehill.com/blogs/blog-briefing-room/4081551-smallville-actress-sentenced-in-nxivm-sex-cult-case-secures-early-release-from-prison/.

32. Jiwon Song, "A South Korean Religious Sect Leader Has Been Sentenced to 23 Years in Prison Over Sex Crimes," AP News, December 22, 2023, https://apnews.com/article/south-korea-jms-jung-myung-seok-prison-e712f5c3a26f6aaca3558c6f8f49ffb1.

Chapter 2

1. "Imposter Syndrome: Definition, symptoms & Tips to Overcome it," BetterUp, n.d., https://www.betterup.com/blog/what-is-imposter-syndrome-and-how-to-avoid-it.
2. Luciana Paulise, "75% of women executives experience imposter syndrome in the workplace," *Forbes*, August 3, 2023, https://www.forbes.com/sites/lucianapaulise/2023/03/08/75-of-women-executives-experience-imposter-syndrome-in-the-workplace/.
3. Dexter Tilo, "Searches for Impostor Syndrome surge 75% in 2024," HRD America, February 8, 2024, https://www.hcamag.com/us/specialization/mental-health/searches-for-impostor-syndrome-surge-75-in-2024/476335.
4. Cheri Beranek, "Imposter Syndrome Predominantly Affects Women—Here's How We Can Overcome It," *Entrepreneur*, June 14, 2023, https://www.entrepreneur.com/leadership/imposter-syndrome-predominantly-affects-women-heres/453161.
5. SWNS, "This is how often a person typically feels insecure: poll," *New York Post*, March 31, 2023, https://nypost.com/2023/03/30/this-is-how-often-a-person-typically-feels-insecure-poll/.
6. Joyce Marter, LCPC, "5 Types of Imposter Syndrome & How to Overcome Them," Choosing Therapy, May 23, 2023, https://www.choosingtherapy.com/imposter-syndrome-types/.
7. "Imposter Syndrome: Definition, symptoms & Tips to Overcome it." BetterUp, February 22, 2023, https://www.betterup.com/blog/what-is-imposter-syndrome-and-how-to-avoid-it.
8. Kendra Cherry, "How multitasking affects productivity and brain health," Verywell Mind, March 1, 2023, https://www.verywellmind.com/multitasking-2795003.
9. Kess Eruteya, "You're not an imposter. you're actually pretty amazing," *Harvard Business Review*, July 23, 2023, https://hbr.org/2022/01/youre-not-an-imposter-youre-actually-pretty-amazing.
10. Julia Martins, "Unmasking impostor syndrome: 15 ways to overcome it at work," Asana, May 31, 2024, https://asana.com/resources/impostor-syndrome

Chapter 3

1. Barnum Financial Group, "The confidence gap: what it is, where it's from, and what we can do," August 27, 2021, https://barnumfinancial-group.com/the-confidence-gap-what-it-is-where-its-from-and-what-we-can-do.

2. Vanessa Fillis and Mafe Callejón, "A visual exploration of gender inequality statistics in 2024," Flourish, March 8, 2024, https://flourish.studio/blog/international-womens-day.

3. Darya Sinusoid, "Women and Confidence: Why they Lack Self-Faith," Shortform Books, September 6, 2021, https://www.shortform.com/blog/women-and-confidence/.

4. Katie Doll, "The 2 biggest side effects of overthinking in women," Shortform Books, October 15, 2023, https://www.shortform.com/blog/side-effects-of-overthinking.

5. Bailey Reiners, "What Is the Glass Ceiling?" Built In, November 7, 2023, https://builtin.com/diversity-inclusion/glass-ceiling.

6. Jaclyn Margolis, "Overlooked Reasons Why Women Don't Get Promoted," Psychology Today, April 28, 2023, https://www.psychologytoday.com/ca/blog/shifting-workplace-dynamics/202304/overlooked-reasons-why-women-dont-get-promoted.

7. Manasa Ramakrishnan, "What is the Broken Rung and Why Corporate Leadership Must Fix it," Emeritus, March 24, 2023, https://emeritus.org/blog/leadership-broken-rung.

8. Emily Field, Alexis Krivkovich, Sandra Kügele, Nicole Robinson, and Lareina Yee, "Women in the Workplace 2023," McKinsey & Company, October 5, 2023, https://www.mckinsey.com/featured-insights/diversity-and-inclusion/women-in-the-workplace.

9. Benjamin Lee, "Study shows 'catastrophic' 10-year low for female representation in film," Guardian, February 21, 2024, https://www.theguardian.com/film/2024/feb/21/female-representation-film-usc-annenberg-study.

10. National Organization for Women, "Get the Facts," n.d., https://now.org/now-foundation/love-your-body/love-your-body-whats-it-all-about/get-the-facts.

11. Zahaab Rehman, "25 Worst Countries for Gender Equality," Yahoo Finance, March 17, 2024, https://finance.yahoo.com/news/25-worst-countries-gender-equality-005627134.html.

12. Register Staff, "Full text: Harrison Butker of Kansas City Chiefs graduation speech," *NCR*, May 16, 2024, https://www.ncregister.com/news/harrison-butker-speech-at-benedictine.

13. Benedictine College, "Tuition & Fee Schedule," n.d., https://www.benedictine.edu/Assets/uploads/files/admission/annual-semester-tuition-fees.pdf.

14. John Helton, "Benedictine College nuns denounce Harrison Butker's speech at their school," *NPR*, May 19, 2024, https://www.npr.org/2024/05/19/1252357764/harrison-butker-benedictine-college-commencement-nuns-denounce.

15. https://www.facebook.com/mountosb/posts/pfbid0k1kb7TE8ycyMJDbFPwrnjipkyUjGofh9BTctzxBa9U5QAQTKQ2NmFyaqf71WWGKbl.

16. "Over one million women now in STEM occupations but still account for 29% of STEM workforce," Institution of Engineering and Technology, March 8, 2024, https://www.theiet.org/media/press-releases/press-releases-2024/press-releases-2024-january-march/8-march-2024-over-one-million-women-now-in-stem-occupations-but-still-account-for-29-of-stem-workforce.

17. Member News, "Filling the Gap: The Effects of the 'Confidence Gap' in STEM and 3 Ways to Fix It," All Together, December 2, 2021, https://alltogether.swe.org/2021/12/filling-the-gap-the-effects-of-the-confidence-gap-in-stem-and-3-ways-to-fix-it/.

18. Emma Parker, Bryan Gerson, and Michael Baynes, 50 Women in Business Statistics in 2024, Clarify Capital, https://clarifycapital.com/women-in-business-statistics.

19. Emilia Vidadievna, "Does Gender in Entrepreneurship Still Matter in 2024," AI Bees, June 12, 2024, https://www.ai-bees.io/post/gender-in-entrepreneurship-does-it-still-matter.

20. Surveillance video shows Sean 'Diddy' Combs physically assaulting former girlfriend in 2016, CNN, May 17, 2024, https://www.cnn.com/2024/05/17/entertainment/video/sean-diddy-combs-cassie-venture-surveillance-digvid.

21. Zach Sharf, "Cassie Thanks Fans for Support After Release of Diddy Assault Video: 'Domestic Violence Is the Issue. . .Open Your Heart to Believing Victims the First Time,'" *Variety*, May 23, 2024, https://

variety.com/2024/music/news/cassie-statement-diddy-hotel-assault-video-1236014370/.

22. NCADV, National Coalition against Domestic Violence, (n.d.), https://ncadv.org/STATISTICS.

23. Erin Blakemore, "How classic Hollywood's party culture turned women into prey," History Channel, May 5, 2023, https://www.history .com/news/sexual-abuse-in-old-hollywood-mgm-stag-party.

Chapter 4

1. Richard Zinbarg, "The Meaning of Courage," *Psychology Today*, November 11, 2010, https://www.psychologytoday.com/us/blog/cultivating-courage/201011/the-meaning-courage.

2. Mind Tools Content Team, "5 Whys, Mind Tools," Mind Tools, n.d., https://www.mindtools.com/a3mi00v/5-whys.

3. Gayle MacBride, "Important tips for effective self-talk," Alina Health, July 23, 2015, https://www.allinahealth.org/healthysetgo/thrive/important-tips-for-effective-selftalk.

4. Emily DiNuzzo, "16 Famous 'Failures' of Wildly Successful People," *Reader's Digest*, July 17, 2024, https://www.rd.com/list/ironic-failures-of-wildly-successful-people.

5. "6 Women Entrepreneurs Who Failed Before Succeeding," WECAN, October 8, 2021, https://wecanmag.com/6-women-entrepreneurs-who-failed-before-succeeding/.

Chapter 5

1. Teresa Nowakowski, "'*Barbie* Makes History, Becoming First Billion-Dollar Movie Directed Solely by a Woman," *Smithsonian Magazine*, August 9, 2023, https://www.smithsonianmag.com/smart-news/barbie-first-billion-dollar-movie-directed-by-a-woman-180982672.

2. Psychology Today Staff, "Self-Sabotage," *Psychology Today*, n.d., https://www.psychologytoday.com/ca/basics/self-sabotage.

3. Allaya Cooks-Campbell, "How to stop self-sabotaging: 5 steps to change your behavior," BetterUp, April 12, 2022, https://www .betterup.com/blog/how-to-stop-self-sabotaging.

4. Justin Firth and Neha Veyas, "What role do cultural differences play in self-promotion?" INvolve, May 30, 2023, https://www.involvepeople.org/what-role-do-cultural-differences-play-in-self-promotion/.

5. APA *Dictionary of Psychology*, American Psychological Association, (n.d.), https://dictionary.apa.org/cultural-norm.

6. Shobha Rana Grover, "9 Customs That Oppress Women Across the World," HuffPost, March 22, 2017, https://www.huffpost.com/entry/nine-customs-that-oppress-women-across-the-world_b_58d2b18de4b002482d6e6d55.

7. Morgan Smith, "Burnout is on the rise worldwide—and Gen Z, young millennials and women are the most stressed," CNBC, March 14, 2023, https://www.cnbc.com/2023/03/14/burnout-is-on-the-rise-gen-z-millennials-and-women-are-the-most-stressed.html.

8. *The Tao of Self-Confidence*, Listen Notes, n.d., https://www.listennotes.com/podcasts/the-tao-of-self-confidence-sheena-yap-chan-X0IkteTno7r.

9. Seth Berkman, "Korean TV's Unlikely Star: Subway Sandwiches," *New York Times*, March 14, 2021, https://www.nytimes.com/2021/03/14/business/media/subway-product-placement-korea.html.

10. Sophie Haigney, "Anatomy of a Product Placement," *New York Times*, June 24, 2022, https://www.nytimes.com/interactive/2022/06/23/arts/product-placement.html.

Chapter 6

1. SWNS, "Half of women believe they're just entering their 'confidence era'," *New York Post*, 2023, 13 October https://nypost.com/2023/10/13/half-of-women-believe-theyre-just-entering-their-confidence-era.

2. Kendra Cherry, "How Neuroplasticity Works," Verywell Mind, May 17, 2024, https://www.verywellmind.com/what-is-brain-plasticity-2794886.

3. Calm, "Visualization meditation: 8 exercises to add to your practice," n.d., https://www.calm.com/blog/visualization-meditation.

4. Elyse Stoltz Dickerson, "Advice from a Female CEO: How to Build Confidence in and out of the Office," *Forbes*, June 27, 2020, https://www.forbes.com/sites/womensmedia/2020/06/27/advice-from-a-female-ceo-how-to-build-confidence-in-and-out-of-the-office.

5. General Staff, "7 inspiring stories of women in business to encourage and uplift you," Invoice2Go, n.d., https://invoice.2go.com/blog/inspiring-stories-women-in-business/#lhijcs603d-

6. Michelle Martin, "Learning to Trust Your Women's Intuition," HuffPost, June 6, 2016, https://www.huffpost.com/entry/womens-intuition_b_10192222.

Chapter 7

1. Brandee Sanders, "5 Things to Know About the Life and Times of Uptown Trailblazer Yuri Kochiyama," Columbia Neighbors, May 10, 2023, https://neighbors.columbia.edu/news/5-things-know-about-life-and-times-uptown-trailblazer-yuri-kochiyama.

2. Eleanor Roosevelt's Life, PBS, (n.d.), https://www.pbs.org/wgbh/americanexperience/features/Eleanor-timeline-eleanor-biography/.

3. Life in the Red Room, The White House - George W. Bush, (n.d.), https://georgewbush-whitehouse.archives.gov/history/life/redroom.html.

4. Life Story: Sarah "Madam C.J." Breedlove Walker (1867–1919), Women & The American Story, (n.d.), https://wams.nyhistory.org/modernizing-america/modern-womanhood/madam-cj-walker/.

5. Maria Eva Peron, Iowa State University, (n.d.), https://awpc.cattcenter.iastate.edu/directory/eva-peron/.

6. Solomon Amar, Why Everyone Wins With More Women In Leadership, *Forbes*, Feb 7, 2023, https://www.forbes.com/sites/forbesbusinesscouncil/2023/02/07/why-everyone-wins-with-more-women-in-leadership/.

7. Jeanne Sahadi, "Share of women in C-suite roles falls for first time in two decades, study finds," CNN, April 5, 2024, https://www.cnn.com/2024/04/05/success/gender-parity-women-corporate-leaders/index.html.

8. Brian Stone, Companies with female CEOs found to be more profitable on average, Tech Republic, June 1, 2022, https://www.techrepublic.com/article/companies-with-female-ceos-found-to-be-more-profitable-on-average/.

9. Paige Minemyer, "CVS reports double-digit revenue growth in 2022, $4.1B in profit," Fierce Healthcare, February 8, 2023, https://www .fiercehealthcare.com/payers/cvs-reports-double-digit-revenue-growth-2022-41b-profit.

10. Frank Diamond, CVS cuts 2024 outlook amid rise in medical costs in Q4, Fierce Healthcare, February 7, 2024, https://www.fiercehealthcare .com/payers/cvs-earns-350-billion-revenue-2023-over-77-billion-profit.

11. Karen S. Lynch, U.S. News, (n.d.), https://www.usnews.com/news/ live-events/karen-s-lynch.

12. Homeownership Is Harder Than Ever—But This CEO Is Making It Possible, The New Era of Leadership, (n.d.), https://thenewera.chief .com/winners/priscilla-almodovar/.

13. Chris, Slow, "Fannie Mae 2023 financials cap off 'successful' year, CEO says," Housing Wire, February 15, 2024, https://www .housingwire.com/articles/fannie-mae-2023-financials-cap-off-successful-year-ceo-says/.

14. CNBC Staff, "CNBC Changemakers - Thasunda Brown Duckett," CNBC, February 28, 2024, https://www.cnbc.com/2024/02/28/ thasunda-brown-duckett-cnbc-changemakers.html.

15. Council Post, "20 Strategies To Keep Women In The C-Suite," *Forbes*, February 21, 2024, https://www.forbes.com/sites/forbeshu manresourcescouncil/2024/02/21/20-strategies-to-keep-women-in-the-c-suite/.

16. Facts and figures: Women's leadership and political participation, UN Women, (n.d.), https://www.unwomen.org/en/what-we-do/leadership-and-political-participation/facts-and-figures.

17. Michael E. Miller, "Ardern's covid policy was her 'greatest legacy' — but also her undoing," *Washington Post*, January 20, 2023, https:// www.washingtonpost.com/world/2023/01/20/jacinda-ardern-new-zealand-covid-resignation/.

18. Helen Davidson, "Taiwan hits zero Covid cases for first time since outbreak in May," *Guardian*, August 25, 2021, https://www .theguardian.com/world/2021/aug/25/taiwan-zero-covid-cases-out break-vaccine-test-trace.

19. Jon Henley, "Are female leaders more successful at managing the coronavirus crisis?" *Guardian*, April 25, 2020, https://www .theguardian.com/world/2020/apr/25/why-do-female-leaders-seem-to-be-more-successful-at-managing-the-coronavirus-crisis.

20. Silvana Koch-Mehrin and Dominik Weh, "Countries with more women in government are more prosperous," World Economic Forum, November 15, 2023, https://www.weforum.org/agenda/2023/11/women-government-representation/.

21. Ibid.

22. Five Effective Ways to Involve Women in Politics, UNDP, February 21, 2021, https://www.undp.org/ukraine/news/five-effective-ways-involve-women-politics.

23. Annie Kelly and Zahra Joya, "'Frightening' Taliban law bans women from speaking in public," *The Guardian*, August 26, 2024, https://www.theguardian.com/global-development/article/2024/aug/26/taliban-bar-on-afghan-women-speaking-in-public-un-afghanistan.

24. New Report Finds Growth of Women Business Owners Outpaces the Market, Wells Fargo, January 9, 2024, https://newsroom.wf.com/English/news-releases/news-release-details/2024/New-Report-Finds-Growth-of-Women-Business-Owners-Outpaces-the-Market/.

25. 5 Challenges Faced By Women Entrepreneurs & What To Do, Boopos, May 9, 2024, https://www.boopos.com/all-post/challenges-women-entrepreneur.

26. Christina Sanders, "2024 Woman-Owned Business Statistics, lendio, March 22, 2024, https://www.lendio.com/blog/women-business-statistics/.

27. Samantha Kroontje, "The Richest Women In The World 2024," *Forbes*, April 2, 2024, https://www.forbes.com/sites/samanthakroontje/2024/04/02/the-richest-women-in-the-world-francoise_bettencourt-meyers-taylor-swift-alice-walton-2024/.

28. Chase Peterson-Withorn, "Forbes 38th Annual World's Billionaires List: Facts And Figures 2024," *Forbes*, April 2, 2024, https://www .forbes.com/sites/chasewithorn/2024/04/02/forbes-38th-annual-worlds-billionaires-list-facts-and-figures-2024/.

29. Natalie Wu, "The World's Richest Self-Made Women In 2024," *Forbes*, April 3, 2024, https://www.forbes.com/sites/nataliewu/2024/04/03/the-worlds-richest-self-made-women-in-2024-taylor-swift-kim-kardashian-rihanna/.

30. Sarah Bregel, "Elon Musk's attack on MacKenzie Scott's philanthropy reveals our bigger problem with women billionaires," *Fast Company*, March 7, 2024, https://www.fastcompany.com/91050644/elon-musk-mackenzie-scott-bezos-philanthropy-tweet-criticism-women-billio naires.

31. Melody Chiu, "Taylor Swift Gives Bonuses Totaling Over $55 Million to Every Person Working on Massive Eras Tour," *People*, August 2, 2023, https://people.com/taylor-swift-gives-bonuses-totaling-55-million-every-person-working-eras-tour-7568556.

32. Hannah Dailey and Rania Aniftos, "A Timeline of Taylor Swift's Generosity," *Billboard*, February 16, 2024, https://www.billboard.com/lists/taylor-swifts-charity-donations-gifts-timeline.

33. Elizabeth Ralph, "Why women give away more money," *Politico*, December 18, 2020, https://www.politico.com/newsletters/women-rule/2020/12/18/why-women-give-away-more-money-491197.

34. David A. Fahrenthold and Ryan Mac, "Elon Musk Has a Giant Charity. Its Money Stays Close to Home," *New York Times*, March 10, 2024, https://www.nytimes.com/2024/03/10/us/elon-musk-charity.html.

Chapter 8

1. Sue Duke, "Why we must act now to revive women's leadership prospects in an AI-driven workplace," World Economic Forum, June 12, 2024, https://www.weforum.org/agenda/2024/06/how-an-ai-driven-future-can-include-more-women-in-leadership.

Acknowledgments

THERE ARE SO many people I would like to thank for making this book possible. First, I would like to thank Wiley for giving me the opportunity to write this book and the previous book, *The Tao of Self-Confidence*. You have shown what is possible for me because being an author was not something I had on my vision board. You have shown me what I am capable of, and I am grateful for that every single day.

I would like to thank my family for always being there for me through thick and thin. Thank you to my parents; my sisters, Phoebe, Tootsie, and Ellen; my brother-in-law, Roger; and my nieces and nephews, Mehgan, Shanaia, Cayton, Nolan, and Jonah.

I would like to thank my amazing friends who have also been there for me through thick and thin. Thank you to my girls in Toronto, Maureen, Aileen, Nicole, Mae, and Sabrina, for your friendship over the years. To my WLG crew, Diane, Melissa, Jovita, Khonie, Celina, and Lynel, I am so grateful that we have been able to keep in touch and that you are still my barkada even if we're miles apart.

I would like to thank the following groups who have supported me in my journey. Without your support, I wouldn't be here today. Thank you to the Women Who BossUp movement for helping me BOSS UP in my own journey. Thank you to USPAACC-WISE for the guidance and support you have given me; it truly means a lot to be in this group and sisterhood. Thank you to CAPAW for the support you have given me to always show up as a leader. Thank you to the Femmefluence family for the support and excitement for the impact we will create together. Last but not least, thank you to my Tao Queens and Queen Makers team for creating this tribe of queens and leaders that will create a *big* impact in the world. I am forever grateful for you!

And of course I want to thank *you* for your continued support over the years. Without your support, this would not happen. I am always grateful that you believe in me and my message. It's because of you that I continue to move forward! Thank you, thank you, thank you!

About the Author

Sheena Yap Chan is a corporate trainer, a *Wall Street Journal* best-selling author, keynote speaker, strategist, corporate trainer, and award-winning podcaster renowned for her expertise in elevating leadership and self-confidence through media. She is the founder and host of the acclaimed podcast *The Tao of Self-Confidence*, where she interviews women about their journeys to self-confidence. With over one million downloads, her podcast ranks among the top 0.5% most popular shows globally and features over 800 interviews, including conversations with celebrities and eight-figure CEOs.

Sheena's influence extends beyond podcasting. Her debut book, *The Tao of Self-Confidence: A Guide to Moving Beyond Trauma and Awakening the Leader Within*, published by Wiley, is a *Wall Street Journal* and *Publishers Weekly* bestseller. It is also recognized as one of the top 20 best self-confidence books of all time by Book Authority, the world's leading site for book recommendations. Her work has been featured on prominent platforms such as MindValley, FOX, NBC News, and the *Manila Times*.

Sheena is dedicated to bridging the gender confidence gap through her training and programs, aiming to elevate women into leadership roles across all industries. She has delivered impactful speeches for organizations like Live Nation, NASA, and UKG, sharing her insights on self-confidence and leadership. She is also the co-founder of TAO Queens and Queenmaker.ai, a community for women dedicated to unleashing their inner queen.

You can connect with Sheena through her websites https://sheenayapchan.com, https://thetaoofselfconfidence.com, https://taoqueens.com, and https://queenmaker.ai/.

Index

ALSO FROM
SHEENA
YAP CHAN

The Wall Street Journal
BESTSELLER

The

Tao

of

Self-
Confidence

A GUIDE TO MOVING BEYOND TRAUMA
AND AWAKENING THE LEADER WITHIN

Sheena Yap Chan

WILEY

The Tao of Self-Confidence • ISBN: 978-1-394-16657-2

WILEY